OPERATION

THE IRANIAN EMBASSY SIEGE

RUSSELL PHILLIPS

SHILKA PUBLISHING
WWW.SHILKA.CO.UK

Shilka Publishing
Apt 2049
Chynoweth House
Trevissome Park
Truro
TR4 8UN
www.shilka.co.uk

Book Layout ©2013 BookDesignTemplates.com

Ordering Information:
Quantity sales. Special discounts are available on quantity purchases by corporations, associations, and others. For details, contact the "Special Sales Department" at the address above.

Operation Nimrod/ Russell Phillips. —1st ed.
ISBN 978-0-9927648-8-3

CONTENTS

"The soldier always knows that everything he does on such an occasion will be scrutinised by two classes of critics — by the Government which employs him and by the enemies of that Government. As far as the Government is concerned, he is a little Admiral Jellicoe and this is his tiny Battle of Jutland. He has to make a vital decision on incomplete information in a matter of seconds, and afterwards the experts can sit down at leisure with all the facts before them, and argue about what he might, could, or should have done. Lucky the soldier if, as in Jellicoe's case, the tactical experts decided after twenty years' profound consideration that what he did in three minutes was right. As for the enemies of the Government, it does not much matter what he has done. They will twist, misinterpret, falsify, or invent any fact as evidence that he is an inhuman monster wallowing in innocent blood".

—Field Marshal Sir William Slim, Unofficial History

30th April 1980: Day 1

On the morning of Wednesday, 30th April 1980, six men left their flat in Kensington, London. They told the landlord that they were spending a week in Bristol before leaving for Iraq, and that they would not be returning. They had made arrangements for their belongings to be sent on ahead of them, they said. The men were Khuzestani revolutionaries, and although they'd spent the previous few weeks enjoying London's bustling nightlife and buying consumer goods, that was simply some downtime before the primary mission, which was about to begin.

The men collected two submachine guns, four automatic pistols, a revolver, ammunition, and hand grenades. They carried the weapons in lightweight holdalls as they walked to their target, the Iranian embassy at 16 Princes Gate in Knightsbridge. It is believed the weapons had entered the UK in an Iraqi diplomatic bag. The men had received a little training in the use of the firearms from the Iraqi army, but they were not particularly competent. Neither the Khuzestanis nor the Iraqis believed that this would be an issue. Pitched gunfights with the British authorities were not part of the plan: British police weren't armed, after all.

One man, Themir Moammed Hussein (Later code named "Abbas" by the police) went on ahead to do a last reconnaissance. He was a squat, heavily-built individual, with scars on each cheek. The others waited at the Albert Memorial, and when Abbas returned he told them that all was well. He estimated that at least twenty-five people were inside the target. Twenty-five people to use as hostages, their safety to be bargained for in return for the men's demands. The leader, Oan Ali Mohammed (code named "Salim"), gave the order to start the attack, and all six men headed towards the embassy. After leaving Hyde Park, they split up. Salim, his second-in-command Shakir Abdullah Radhil ("Faisal"), and Abbas turned left out of the park, looping around to approach their target from the east. The other three, Shakir Sultan Said ("Hassan"), Fowzi Badavi Nejad ("Ali"), and Makki Hanoun Ali ("Makki") approached from the west.

As they approached the embassy, the men were surprised to note that there was no police officer on duty at the entrance. On each of their previous reconnaissance missions they had seen a policeman, one of the Metropolitan Police's Diplomatic Protection Group (DPG), outside the building. Today, there was no policeman. This was obviously divine intervention, signalling that their mission was blessed. They pulled hoods and kaffiyehs around their heads, drew their weapons and made them ready. Faisal shouted "Long live Arabistan", and they ran into the building, Salim in the lead.

PC Trevor Lock was the policeman who should have been stood outside the door as the terrorists approached. It wasn't his shift, but he'd agreed to cover for a colleague. It was a cold day, and Lock had stepped inside to accept an offer of a warm coffee at exactly the wrong time. To make matters worse, the inner security door had been left open due to a large number of visitors entering and leaving the building that morning.

At 11:25, the terrorists ran in. Lock was stood in the entrance hall, near the door to reception. Salim ran towards him, yelling "Don't move!" in Farsi and firing a burst from his submachine gun. Lock was carrying a .38 Smith & Wesson Model 10 revolver in a holster on his right hip, but was unable to draw it before he was overcome. He did manage to use his panic button to transmit an emergency signal, before Salim ripped the radio from his tunic.

Alerted by Lock's emergency signal, four armed policemen on motorbikes were at the embassy within minutes, shortly followed by two sergeants and seven constables of the DPG. The policemen moved around the outside of the embassy, trying to ascertain exactly what had happened. One, approaching the rear, saw a terrorist at a first-floor window and shouted up to ask who he was and what he wanted. The only answer was a warning not to come closer, and so the policeman retreated.

Meanwhile, Abbas Fallahi, the embassy's doorman, and Simeon (Sim) Harris, a BBC sound recordist visiting the embassy to obtain a visa, were immediately captured. They were told to stand against a wall along with Lock, who was bleeding from a cut on his cheek. Hassan and Makki guarded these three hostages while the others started to investigate the rest of the building. Salim assured them that they had nothing to worry about, that they only wanted to "make a few speeches". When he pulled a hand grenade from his pocket and put a finger in the pull-ring, the three hostages became sure that he wasn't telling them the truth.

Chris Cramer, a BBC news producer and Harris' colleague, had run into another room, hoping to escape through a window, but was unable to open it. He was herded out and into the hall with four other men. The eight hostages were taken to the cipher room (room 9A) on the second floor, where Makki stood guard over them. The other terrorists combed the building, yelling, kicking open doors, and rounding up the rest of the building's occupants.

Dr Gholam-Ali Afrouz, the Chargé d'Affaires, was in his first-floor office, giving an interview to Muhammad Faruqi, a London-based journalist. As a staunch supporter of the Ayatollah, Afrouz was a prime target for the terrorists. He was also acutely aware of the possibility of an attack. Just days before, he had written to Chief Superintendent Bromley of the Diplomatic Protection Group. The letter sought to bring to Bromley's attention "the increasing threats our embassy and Diplomatic staff are being confronted with under the present circumstances"[1]. Afrouz wanted to "stress the seriousness of this matter and draw [his] special attention to any stricter precautions". Bromley's response, which had arrived the previous day, offered platitudes but little substance, assuring Afrouz that "the varying political climate together with the need for any additional security precautions are constantly under review"[2].

Afrouz and Faruqi weren't aware of the attack until two men started shouting Afrouz's name from just outside the door. Afrouz locked the door; and the two men tried to break it down but soon gave up, unaware who was in the room. When they moved on, Afrouz unlocked the door, went to the back of the building, and jumped from a window. His attempted escape failed, however, as the impact knocked him out, broke his jaw, and injured his right arm and ribs. Faruqi had not moved. A terrorist found him shortly after and escorted him up to the second floor, where he joined the other hostages being guarded by Makki.

A group of embassy staff and Mustapha Karkouti, a Syrian journalist, took refuge in an office on the fourth floor, locking it from the inside. They waited in silence until one of the women, unable to control herself, started to scream. One of the other women slapped her across the face. The shock stopped the screaming, but it was too late: Salim burst in, firing his submachine gun into the ceiling. They were taken down to the second floor, where they joined the other hostages in the cipher room.

---

[1] The National Archives (TNA): FCO 8/3661
[2] TNA: FCO 8/3661

Ron Morris, the British manager of the embassy, was in his fourth-floor office. Hearing the noise and believing it to be a student demonstration, he decided to investigate. As he headed downstairs, he saw two armed men leading Lock and Fallahi. Turning, he ran back to his office to call 999. Before he could get through, Faisal burst into the room and ordered Morris to go with him.

Morris was the last of the hostages to be caught. As he entered the cipher room, the terrorists ordered the hostages into the adjacent room (room nine). Although this new room was significantly larger, there still wasn't very much space. It was filled with filing cabinets, desks, and other office furniture. Hassan leaped onto a desk and pulled a phone cable out of the wall, before throwing the telephone itself against the wall. Cramer, stubbing his cigarette out, offered one to Salim and asked what he intended to do with the hostages. Salim's voice was gentle, but he refused to answer, and ordered two of the terrorists to search them. The search wasn't very thorough. Faisal noticed a bulge in PC Lock's pocket, but Lock was able to convince him that it was just some notebooks and maps. By this remarkable deception, he was able to keep his revolver.

Not everyone in the embassy had been captured; two people had managed to climb out of a ground-floor window. They had then run across the street and called the police. One embassy official had climbed from a first-floor balcony onto the balcony of the adjacent Ethiopian embassy, where the surprised staff had let him inside. Dr Gholam-Ali Afrouz, the Chargé d'Affaires, was still unconscious at the back of the embassy after his attempted escape. One of the hostages noticed him lying on the floor. Thinking he was dead, several of the hostages started to weep, adding to the tension in the room. PC Lock tried to calm them down, saying that he believed the terrorists were only firing blanks.

Having spotted Afrouz, two terrorists went to get him, reaching him just as he started to come around. Still in a lot of pain from his injuries, he was dragged upstairs. As the highest-ranking hostage and a known supporter of Ayatollah Khomeini, Afrouz became a primary target for the terrorist's ire. He was initially held separately, but later dumped in the same room as the other hostages, where he collapsed, unable to stand. Morris shouted at the terrorists to call a doctor, but Salim refused and told Morris to be quiet. Morris did manage to get some water, which he used to clean Afrouz's face, and Cramer also used it to clean the wounds on PC Lock's face. Lock showed Cramer his hidden revolver, telling the BBC man to take it if anything happened to him. Realising that Cramer had never used a gun, Lock explained that there was no safety catch. All Cramer would have to do was aim and pull the trigger.

As the atmosphere slowly calmed, some of the hostages started to wonder if anyone knew what had happened to them. Salim disappeared, and when he came back, he was carrying a large bundle of leaflets, one of which he handed to Cramer. He told the hostages that he was going to tell them why the terrorists had taken the embassy and what they wanted. He would read in Farsi, then Cramer would read in English. The message started with an apology to the British people and government for any inconvenience. It went on to demand the release of ninety-one Arab prisoners held in Arabistan, an aeroplane to fly the terrorists out of the UK, and recognition of Arabistan as an autonomous region. It stated that the embassy would be blown up if the British government did not react within twenty-four hours.

Cramer asked how they intended to get their demands to the outside world, and Salim responded that they had thrown leaflets to the police outside. If they didn't hear anything within twenty-four hours, he added, the hostages would be killed.

At this point, the police had very little information. They knew hostages had been taken, but they didn't know how many, nor did they know the number or nature of the hostage takers. It was unclear whether the situation was a normal criminal matter, or if it had a political dimension that would require government involvement. Those officials who might be needed (ironically, some of them were attending a conference on terrorism) were warned and put on standby.

The Foreign and Commonwealth Office (FCO) was concerned that reprisals might be taken against the British embassy in Tehran. A flash telegram was sent, warning them to take precautions. A further message, addressed from Lord Carrington, the Foreign Secretary, was to be delivered to Iranian President Bani-Sadr. This expressed the foreign secretary's "deep personal concern" and hope that the situation would be resolved swiftly, with the hostages' lives as a "paramount consideration". The message was also sent to Abu Dhabi, to be delivered to the Iranian foreign minister, who was visiting the United Arab Emirates.

At 11:45, the terrorists threw leaflets, written in Farsi, out of a window. By this time, Chief Superintendent Bromley of the DPG was on the scene. Salim shouted a summary of their demands, in English, to the police from a window. He told the police that they were the Group of the Martyr. They demanded the release of ninety-one prisoners held in Iran, recognition of Arabistan as an autonomous region, and an aeroplane to take the terrorists and hostages out of Britain once the prisoners had been released. The police were told that the hostages would be killed if the demands were not met within twenty-four hours, and the embassy would be blown up if a rescue attempt was mounted.

Now that the nature of the incident was known to be political, the government needed to be involved. Arrangements were made to set up the Cabinet Office Briefing Room (COBR, pronounced "cobra"). COBR sits in times of emergency, and is chaired by the home secretary, with senior MOD, Cabinet Office, and Foreign Office ministers. In political hostage situations, the Metropolitan Police,

MI5, and SAS are also represented on COBR. In this way, the SAS have access to the people making decisions and can advise them accordingly.

One policeman who heard the calls on the radio was PC Dusty Gray, recently retired from the SAS. Knowing the regiment's hostage-rescue role, he realised that they might be needed, so he called the regimental headquarters in Hereford. He was put through to Lieutenant-Colonel Rose, the regiment's commanding officer. Rose, knowing that Gray had a reputation for practical jokes, was initially sceptical. He called Brigadier Peter de la Billière, Director SAS Group, at the Ministry of Defence (MOD), for confirmation. While he was waiting for confirmation, he sent a live operation alert to the Special Projects (SP) Team at 11:48. The SP Team was the title given to the squadron currently assigned to the anti-terrorist role. Each of the four SAS sabre squadrons rotated through six-month tours on SP Team duty. When on that duty, they trained in close-quarter combat, hostage-rescue techniques, etc.

B Squadron had recently taken over from D Squadron as the SP Team. The SP Team is split into two independent teams, codenamed Blue Team and Red Team. At any one time, one team is on thirty minutes' notice to deploy, with the other on three hours' notice. Normally the two teams work together, but they could work independently if the situation demanded. Since the whole of 22 SAS Regiment rotate through the SP Team role, other squadrons could be called upon to assist if necessary.

Deputy Assistant Commissioner (DAC) Dellow took over command of the police presence at Princes Gate at noon, and started preparations for a siege. As the police built up their presence, they implemented their standard procedures for such situations. These procedures were known as ICC, an acronym for "Isolate, Cordon, Contain". The police would isolate the incident, cordon off the perimeter, and contain the hostage-takers. Once this was done, they would initiate negotiations, with the hope of reaching a peaceful conclusion. This procedure makes the hostage-takers reliant on the police, since all other outside contact is cut off. A level of trust builds between the hostage-takers and the negotiators. This trust is then used to secure concessions, and ultimately persuade the hostage-takers to give up without harming anyone.

That was the plan. The Metropolitan Police, as well as other police forces elsewhere in the world, had used similar techniques in previous sieges to good effect. On this occasion, however, it was destined to fail.

Dog teams were deployed, in case the terrorists tried to escape. Initially, Dellow planned to set up police headquarters, known as Zulu Control, at Number 25 Princes Gate, which housed the Royal School of Needlework. Although the occupants were willing, it was dismissed as impractical after a few hours. Not only did the building house many priceless artefacts, there was also a strict smoking ban. In 1980, most police officers smoked, and the lack of nicotine soon took its toll. Zulu Control was therefore moved to Number 24, a children's nursery. The only requirements here were that the nursery's pet hamster was to be fed, a duck nesting on a windowsill was not to be disturbed, and the small child-size toilets were to be treated with care.

The police control room was set up in the attic. Police marksmen from D11 — the "Blue Berets" — deployed into positions around the embassy. C11, also known as Special Branch, which works in close conjunction with British intelligence services, and C13, the criminal intelligence and surveillance branch, soon arrived. Officers from C13 started to deploy surveillance and listening equipment. A four-man team of negotiators (later increased to six men) was assembled, with a Farsi interpreter and psychiatrist to support them.

A green field telephone was passed into the Iranian embassy through a downstairs window, on the end of a long wooden pole.

Dellow had ordered the Post Office to cut all telephone and telex lines to the embassy. He wanted the field telephone to be the terrorists' only means of communicating with the outside world. The telephone was very simple, with just two buttons: one to call, and one to speak. What the terrorists didn't know was that the microphone was always live, so that the telephone acted as a bug. In addition, the cable had been discreetly marked so that the police always knew how much was inside the embassy, and therefore which floor the telephone was on.

News of the siege was first broadcast at 12:10, on Independent Radio News (IRN). Simon Prebble, an IRN reporter, had got caught up in the traffic around Princes Gate and had called in with an eyewitness account of the police activity. Other news reporters and TV camera crews soon arrived. They were all herded into an enclosed area which became known as "Pressville", about one hundred yards west of the embassy. There was some concern that television crews might film police preparations, thus giving the terrorists intelligence via the TV news. Attempts to jam television transmissions into the embassy failed, so Dellow ordered the construction of large screens to hide the embassy from TV cameras. In the event, these were not used, in case the terrorists misconstrued them as an attempt to hide preparations for an assault. It's unclear how effective these screens would have been, since all the TV crews acquired hydraulic hoists, giving them a high vantage point.

Senior members of the Ministry of Defence, Foreign Office, Metropolitan Police, Home Office, the Security Service (MI5), and the Secret Intelligence Service (MI6) were summoned to COBR. Brigadier Peter de la Billière, Director SAS Group, attended to represent the SAS. Representatives of the public utilities, gas board, water board, and the British Airports Authority were also called to attend. It took some time to assemble everyone, so COBR didn't convene for the first time until 15:00[3]. The situation was complicated.

---

[3]Margaret Thatcher Foundation archive, document ID 128191

The new Iranian regime was unfriendly to the West. Operation Eagle Claw, an American mission to rescue diplomats held hostage in Tehran, had failed only a few days earlier. Late in the afternoon, an initial response was agreed upon, and this became official UK policy.

No terrorist was to be allowed to leave the UK, under any circumstances.

All terrorists were to be held accountable under UK law.

No hostage would leave the UK under pressure.

The police were to negotiate for as long as was required to reach a peaceful conclusion to the siege.

Although it was hoped that a peaceful conclusion would be reached, an assault by the SAS would be considered if any hostages were wounded.

The SAS would launch an assault if any hostages were killed.

The SAS still hadn't received orders from the MOD to deploy the Special Projects Team, but Lieutenant-Colonel Rose had made the decision to move them to Regent's Park Barracks, where they would prepare for action. Rose himself went ahead, taking a helicopter to RAF Northolt. From there, he drove into London to introduce himself to Dellow and make a preliminary reconnaissance.

Each member of the SP Team had his own dedicated weapons, primarily variants of the Heckler & Koch MP5 submachine gun. Most had the standard model, but there weren't enough to go around, and so a few had the shorter MP5K or the silenced MP5SD. The MP5 is an excellent weapon, with an enviable reputation for both accuracy and reliability. Remington 870 pump-action shotguns were also used, primarily for forced entry through locked doors. Each trooper carried a Browning Hi-Power pistol as a backup weapon. Every man had a holdall containing spare clothing, equipment, and personal kit for use in cases like this. Each vehicle had a pallet of equipment ready to load.

The squadron travelled discreetly in unmarked white Range Rovers. They contacted each area's police force to alert them to their presence as they passed through, but no sirens or blue lights were used. The forward elements arrived at Regent's Park Barracks in the evening of 30th April, with the remainder arriving in the early hours of 1st May.

B Squadron's officers, or "Head Shed" in SAS slang, had left at 14:58, and were briefed at 17:00 at the Defence Situation Centre in London, before moving to Regent's Park Barracks, which was to be the Main Base Station (MBS) for what was now known as Operation Nimrod.

By evening, the police were concerned that the terrorists were becoming unpredictable, and there was a real worry that they might start killing hostages. To ensure a near-instant response time if necessary, the Blue and Red Teams were to alternate twelve-hour shifts on standby. The standby team would be dressed in full assault kit, stationed in the headquarters of the Royal College of General Practitioners, at 14 Princes Gate (nicknamed the "Doctor's House"). The other team would rehearse and plan at Regent's Park Barracks.

While preparations were made for a possible assault, the police had another issue to contend with. Anticipating trouble, the police had set aside an area of Hyde Park to accommodate demonstrators. Several hundred people arrived, both pro-Khomeini and anti-Khomeini. They chanted slogans and pushed against the barriers that had been erected to keep them apart. In addition to the threat of the two groups fighting, the pro-Khomeinis had threatened to storm the embassy and rescue their countrymen. Fighting broke out between the groups, despite the extra policemen deployed to keep them apart. No attempt was made to storm the embassy, however.

Karkouti, the journalist, had suggested to Salim that they should telex the terrorists' demands to his newspaper in Beirut, for them to print. Neither the terrorists nor the hostages knew that the police had ordered the phone and telex lines to be cut. Despite the police order, the telex line was still operational. Salim took Karkouti to the telex room (room ten), warning him not to try anything. When they got to the telex room, they found that a journalist from the Guardian newspaper, John Hooper, was trying to dial in. Salim was suspicious, but Karkouti assured him that the Guardian was a worthwhile newspaper, and likely to print the demands unedited. On Salim's instructions, Karkouti telexed the demands to the Guardian, much to Hooper's delight. The journalist tried to get more information, asking how many terrorists were in the embassy, but Salim refused to respond. Hooper did manage to get a few answers, but when he pushed too far, Salim pulled the power plug out of the socket.

A little later, a report on BBC radio described the terrorists as "Iraqis", which angered Salim. Frieda Mozafarian got very upset, to the point that she vomited into a waste paper bin. Morris, sensing an opportunity, told Salim that she was ill, and that he should let her go. Salim refused, instead using the field telephone to tell the police that they needed a female doctor. The negotiator who answered told him that no doctors were available and suggested that Salim could show his humanity by releasing Mrs Mozafarian. It is a standard tactic in hostage negotiations to suggest that sick captives should be released, and to suggest that doing so would present the hostage-takers in a good light to the rest of the world. Salim refused, but while he was away, the hostages had formulated a plan. The terrorists knew one of the women was pregnant, but not which one. In fact, it was Mrs Hiyech Sanei Kanji, an embassy secretary. Mrs Kanji courageously agreed to allow the other hostages to claim that Mrs Mozafarian was pregnant. They hoped to use this claim to secure Mrs Mozafarian's release.

When Salim returned, PC Lock told him that Mrs Mozafarian was pregnant and sick, and that holding onto her would not help his cause. Salim relented. At 16:30 Hassan and Makki took Mrs Mozafarian downstairs, opened the front door slightly, and pushed her out. She collapsed, screaming. Two policemen came forward to help her to an ambulance, then went with her to the hospital. Following standard operating procedure, the police questioned Mrs Mozafarian, hoping to gain information on the terrorists and the situation inside the embassy. They were disappointed; in her upset state, she claimed not to remember anything.

The mood of the other hostages was improved by Mrs Mozafarian's release. They started introducing themselves to each other, and even made a few jokes. The terrorists were not in a joking mood. Their Iraqi trainers had told them the British authorities would quickly give in to their demands, but it was becoming obvious that this wasn't true. Angry at the inaccuracy of the news reports and the evident lack of police activity, Salim ordered Karkouti to the telex room. He intended to try something new to get their demands to the outside world. He told Karkouti to call the BBC's Arabic Service and tell them to broadcast the group's demands to the Arab world. Karkouti kept calling, but no one answered.

Salim got angry at Karkouti's inability to get through, so Karkouti suggested trying Bush House, home of the BBC World Service. Salim agreed, but warned Karkouti not to try anything. Karkouti got through, and passed on the list of demands. When the journalist started asking questions, Salim broke the connection.

With Salim's agreement, Cramer called BBC TV news direct and gave them the list of demands. Like everyone else, the journalist wanted more information about what was happening inside the embassy. When Cramer started answering questions, Salim took the phone from him and slammed it down.

At 17:30, they tried again. Salim took Karkouti and Cramer to the telex room. Karkouti called the World Service at Bush House, and Cramer called TV news at Shepherd's Bush. Both got through, and passed on the terrorists' demands. Salim told Cramer to say that he had no intention of harming the non-Iranian hostages. Apparently not realising he was contradicting himself, he then threatened to blow up the embassy and everyone inside it if his demands weren't met. A deadline was set for noon the following day (1st May 1980).

The police had a psychiatrist on hand, and at about this time they asked him for an assessment of the terrorists. The psychiatrist, Professor Gunn, was impressed at their stability. Salim, the sole point of contact, appeared to be firm, articulate, and self-confident. Professor Gunn also advised the police that their negotiators were under great stress, and their twelve-hour shifts were too long.

In the evening, the women were taken to the basement kitchens to look for food. They found rice, figs, and pitta bread. It wasn't much, but at least it was something. No one in the embassy had eaten since the assault that morning. Meanwhile, Morris asked for permission to get some cigarettes from his office. Smoking was much more common in 1980 than it is now, and most of the terrorists and hostages were smokers. On the third-floor landing, Morris found a barricade, though he was able to get past it with little difficulty. When he returned, he had two hundred cigarettes, some biscuits, and a bag of sweets.

After eating, Salim took Cramer to the telex room, where he managed to contact the BBC's Deputy Home Editor, Richard Ayre. Salim took the phone, and Ayre recorded the conversation. Salim told Ayre little that was new, but he did say that the hostages would be safe that night.

The female hostages had been trying to get through to the Foreign Ministry in Tehran for some time, and they finally got through at 23:00. Iran's Foreign Minister, Sadegh Ghotbzadeh, was on a foreign visit, and so a deputy took the call. Despite his broken jaw, Afrouz was ordered to pass on the terrorists' demands. Afrouz said that the terrorists were Muslim brothers, and that they only wanted a measure of autonomy, not independence. If the response from Tehran was encouraging, the hostages would be released and the siege ended.

Salim decided that it was time for sleep, and offered Valium to anyone who needed help sleeping. Afrouz had already taken two and fallen asleep, but the others refused them. They were concerned about what might happen during the night, and preferred to remain fully aware.

Without any warning, the terrorists started removing furniture from the room, to set up barricades in the corridors. When a desk drawer fell to the floor, Cramer moved to clear up the contents. Among other things, he found a razor blade and two hat pins, which he kept hidden as potential weapons.

Late that night, Salim got Ghotbzadeh on the phone. He shook Afrouz awake and dragged him into the telex room. Afrouz asked the foreign minister to do as the terrorists wanted. Ghotbzadeh ranted that the terrorists were CIA agents and that the hostages would consider it "an honour and a privilege" to die as martyrs for the Iranian revolution. Salim yelled at Ghotbzadeh and slammed the phone down. Not surprisingly, Ghotbzadeh's response upset the hostages, and some of the women started to cry. Dadgar led some of the Iranians in prayer.

Salim decided that the women should not sleep in the same room as the men, and had the women moved to an adjacent room. Karkouti sat with the British hostages, talking quietly. He told them that he had started negotiating. He didn't think Salim wanted to harm anyone, he just wanted publicity for the plight of his people in Iran. Lock was quiet, obviously worried. He was concerned that by accepting the offer of a hot coffee that morning, he would be blamed for allowing the terrorists to take over the embassy. Harris managed to break Lock out of his musings, and even had him entertaining the other hostages with a collection of dirty jokes.

During the evening, the Iranian Consul General had visited the British Foreign and Commonwealth Office. He provided a key to the embassy and details of the layout, including access points. He also delivered a note verbale, which stated "It is requested that His Excellency the Foreign Secretary will appreciate the severity of the threat and will order the security services to take all possible measures to safeguard their [the hostages'] lives"[4]. The British government took this to mean that they had permission to enter the embassy if necessary. It wasn't until 5th May, however, that they sent a reply making this point: "the Foreign and Commonwealth Office is proceeding on the basis that the embassy's Note constitutes the necessary consent on the part of the embassy for British security authorities to enter the premises of the embassy if they deem it necessary"[5].

The Prime Minister, Mrs Thatcher, was briefed on the situation at 23:30. The police assessment was that the terrorists were calm and likely to remain so for three to four days. The terrorists did not seem to be particularly serious about their demands, so there was some hope of a peaceful, negotiated conclusion. It was not certain whether or not the building had been rigged with explosives. However, it appeared that the terrorists were settling down for the night, and none of the hostages were seriously hurt. Noting that the situation could change quickly and without warning, the prime minister gave DAC Dellow authority to commit the military if an emergency arose and it was not feasible to consult the home secretary.

---

[4] TNA: PREM 19/1137
[5] UK Home Office, Siege of the Iranian embassy – "Official History", Annex D

Political Background

The six terrorists who seized the Iranian embassy were members of the Democratic Revolutionary Front for the Liberation of Arabistan. This group fought for the independence of the area officially named Khuzestan, but known to most inhabitants as Arabistan. Khuzestan is an oil-rich area in southwestern Iran. In 1980 it generated around 10% of the world's — and around 75% of Iran's — oil production. Despite having some degree of autonomy, the people of Khuzestan were never happy with Persian (later Iranian) rule. There is a long history of Khuzestani rebellion against Persian/Iranian rule. After a rebellion in the 1920s, the Shah of Iran began a program of suppression and resettlement of Persians into the area. Dissent was rife throughout the Shah's reign, but whenever it became overt, it was put down with brutal efficiency.

After World War II the Khuzestanis rebelled, seeking independence and closer links to Iraq, but the rebellion was quelled once again. Khuzestan was relatively peaceful until 1978, when local oil workers went on strike, cutting the supply of oil to Tehran. The subsequent reduction in income contributed to the Shah's downfall and the Islamic Revolution of 1979. The regime change did nothing to improve Khuzestan's situation; the Ayatollah was determined that Iran should remain a single, united country. The people of Khuzestan began a violent campaign of unrest. Oil production dropped by around 80%.

Arab governments, particularly Iraq, viewed the new Iranian government with concern. The Ayatollah openly stated that the revolution would be exported. His belief that clerics should rule by divine right was in direct opposition to secular regimes such as that in neighbouring Iraq. Iranian clerics fostered hostility between Persians and Arabs. Tension between Iraq and Iran was furthered by a difference in religion: the population of both Iran and Iraq were largely Shi'a, but Iraq was ruled by Sunnis.

Iran and Iraq entered into a war by proxy, with both sides funding and supporting armed opposition to the other state. Khuzestani groups fighting for greater independence were given training, equipment, and money by Iraq. The six terrorists who seized the Iranian embassy in London had received arms and training from Iraq.

1st May 1980: Day 2

The SAS assault teams had all arrived at Regent's Park Barracks by around 03:00. They found the holding area to be large, draughty, and cold. The toilets were blocked, and there was no hot running water. The one positive was that there were no journalists present. Weapons and equipment were unloaded, and an initial briefing was held.

Once the briefing finished, Red Team went to the Doctor's House to be on-hand for an assault, should that become necessary. Lieutenant Colonel Rose had formulated a very simple Immediate Action (IA) plan. The plan called for the assault teams to enter through as many windows and doors as possible. They would then fight their way through the embassy, using CS gas and stun grenades to keep the terrorists off-balance. The plan relied heavily on speed and aggression. Casualties were likely to be high among both the SAS and the hostages if the plan had to be put into practice. Ultimately, the IA plan was better than no plan at all, but everyone hoped that it wouldn't be needed.

On arriving at the Doctor's House, Red Team conducted a close-target reconnaissance of the Iranian embassy via the roof and balconies. Intelligence officers gathered as much information as they could on the building. Interviews with recent visitors helped to add detail. When the Shah was still in power, the SAS had been asked to advise on security improvements for the embassy. Unfortunately, no one knew which recommendations had been enacted. All of this information was used to draft a new plan. This was the Deliberate Action plan, and it was refined and improved as new information was acquired. To help the soldiers prepare for an assault, police carpenters created a scale model of the embassy, paying careful attention to details such as which direction doors opened.

At Regent's Park Barracks, engineers from the Irish Guards built full-size replicas of each floor of the embassy, enabling the soldiers to rehearse the assault. Again, care was taken with details like doors, since getting them wrong could cost valuable seconds in an assault. Blue Team spent their time training and preparing for an assault. At the Doctor's House, Red Team were on standby. They tried to get some sleep, but since they had to be ready to assault with little or no notice, they wore their assault gear and kept weapons close at all times. The two teams periodically alternated roles. While one rehearsed, the other stood ready to assault as soon as the order was given.

At 05:20, the Iranians said the Fajr prayer as usual. Later, all of the hostages were brought together in room nine, where two of the women volunteered to make breakfast. Salim asked Karkouti to call the BBC again to deliver a message. Karkouti agreed, and got through to Colin Thatcher, a deputy news editor, at 07:02. Karkouti passed on the message that he had been given. It was read out during the 08:00 news: "The Group occupying the Iranian embassy would like to assure the British public opinion [sic] that the British hostages, as well as all other non-Iranian hostages, will not be harmed. They would demonstrate that in a later stage. But the deadline for the safety of the other hostages and the others as well - which is twelve o'clock noon - is still valid. That is all"[6]. Thatcher asked if he could enquire about conditions in the embassy. Karkouti replied that Salim wouldn't allow him to answer questions.

Thatcher persisted. Salim, realising that he had a chance to get his message out to the world, took the phone. Thatcher asked why the group had called for a doctor, and was told that one man was injured. Thatcher asked for details of the injury, but Salim refused. Thatcher discovered that Salim had spoken to the Iranian foreign minister during the night. Salim told Thatcher that "I think he [Ghotbzadeh] will regret this statement"[7]. When Thatcher pressed for clarification, Salim said that he would kill the hostages because "he don't care for the Iranian hostages"[8]. By 09:00, the remaining telex and phone lines had been found and cut. The terrorists were now cut off, and would only be able to talk to anyone outside the embassy with the approval of the police.

Back in room nine, PC Lock refused to eat. He was concerned that if he ate, he might have to go to the toilet. Since he'd be escorted by a terrorist, there was a very real risk that his revolver would be discovered. Cramer also refused food, for a different reason. His stomach felt terrible, and he was alternating between feeling hot and cold. It felt like a recurrence of a bowel disease he'd suffered from during an assignment in Africa. He went to the toilet, but it didn't help. He lay on the floor, with Harris and Karkouti crouched over him, but there was nothing they could do.

While Cramer was lying on the floor, the terrorist Makki got into an argument with Dr Afrouz, the Chargé d'Affaires. Makki told Afrouz to move to another part of the room, and when Afrouz didn't move quickly enough, Makki fired into the ceiling. Cramer picked up the cartridge case ejected from the pistol and put it in his pocket.

---

[6] UK Home Office, Siege of the Iranian embassy – "Official History"
[7] UK Home Office, Siege of the Iranian embassy – "Official History"
[8] UK Home Office, Siege of the Iranian embassy – "Official History"

Although it wasn't immediately obvious how, he thought it might be useful later. The Iranian hostages, fully aware that they were the terrorists' primary target, huddled together and prayed.

By 10:00, Cramer's condition had deteriorated. Salim said that the police had refused his request for a doctor, and asked what medicine Cramer needed. Harris wrote "Lomotil", an anti-diarrhoea medicine, on a piece of paper, and volunteered to talk to the police. Salim led him to the field telephone on the ground floor. Harris asked the negotiator for a doctor, and was told that the request was being considered. Negotiators routinely try to make hostage-takers believe that they are doing their best to help. Delays and problems are blamed on superiors or the authorities — anyone who will help foster the belief that the negotiator is on the side of the terrorist.

When they got back to room nine, Cramer's condition was even worse. Harris told Salim that Cramer needed to get to hospital, and suggested that he release Cramer. Salim had said that he did not mean the British hostages any harm, so surely there was no need to keep him? The terrorists debated among themselves for a few minutes. Having reached a decision, three of them carried the sick man down to the ground floor, placed him on a mattress, and put a blanket over him.

On Salim's orders, Harris called the police once more, with Salim listening in. The negotiator told Harris that they couldn't find a doctor willing to enter the embassy. Harris realised that they were stalling, but didn't tell Salim. When he got back to Cramer, he found Hassan, one of the terrorists, crouched over his sick colleague. There were tears on the terrorist's cheeks.

The terrorists had another discussion; then Salim told Harris that they would release Cramer, as long as he promised not to tell the police anything. Harris assured Salim that Cramer would do as they asked. He was taken back to room nine, leaving Cramer downstairs. Salim took Cramer to the front door and opened it slightly, then told him to go. At 11:15, Chris Cramer walked out of the front door. Two policemen helped him to an ambulance, then followed him in. Despite his promise not to give the police information about the terrorists, Cramer was much more forthcoming than Mrs Mozafarian had been. He told the police that there were six terrorists, with machine guns and grenades, and that PC Lock still had his revolver.

At the hospital, a doctor gave Cramer a check-up and decided that he wasn't seriously ill. The police questioned him, asking about the terrorists, their weapons, and the location of the hostages. Cramer was willing to tell them everything he knew, on condition that the terrorists had no way of knowing that he had helped the police. He also gave them the cartridge case from Makki's pistol.

Although there were no demonstrations in Hyde Park, the mood outside the embassy wasn't completely calm. Three Iranian students were arrested near the Albert Hall, on suspicion of planning to make petrol bombs.

The police also started collecting real-time intelligence. Microphones were lowered down chimneys. Thin holes were drilled in walls to allow tiny video cameras and microphones to be planted. The SAS started to reconnoitre potential entry points. Salim, hearing suspicious noises, asked PC Lock what was causing the sounds. Lock, knowing that it was the police, replied that it was probably mice in the walls. The gas board representative at COBR arranged for the road to be dug up near the embassy under a false pretext, so that the noise would mask that made by the police. Unfortunately, the noise caused problems for the police as well as the terrorists, so the digging was stopped. Instead, air traffic to and from Heathrow was routed over the embassy.

Both the police and the SAS set up sniper teams in positions that overlooked the embassy. The observers in the teams recorded all appearances at windows and doors, detailing as much as possible about the hostages and the terrorists. The information gathered in this way was fed back to the assault teams: the men in those teams had to be able to tell the hostages and terrorists apart. Ideally, they would be able to recognise specific individuals. The intelligence services collated as much information as they could about the terrorists, the group, and the political situation. A large board in the Doctor's House held photographs and as much information as was known about the situation inside the embassy. The SAS troopers spent many hours studying the photographs and committing them to memory.

A little before the deadline expired at noon, Superintendent Luff of Special Branch approached the front of the embassy. Stood behind him, in body armour, was a Farsi interpreter. Luff requested an extension to the deadline, and offered to transmit a message in return. Salim gave this message: "We are giving the Iranian government two more hours, until 2 p.m. today. If the Iranian government will acknowledge that they are negotiating with the British government, that will extend the time. This is not a sign of weakness, but our humanitarian duty. After two o'clock all responsibility falls on the Iranian government"[9].

By this time, Stockholm syndrome, the psychological phenomenon in which hostages empathise and sympathise with their captors, was starting to set in. One of the ways it manifested was in an appeal, written by some of the hostages, on behalf of the terrorists. At 13:09, Salim told the negotiators that he wanted to send a message (the appeal written by the hostages) direct to Tehran via telex. The police were determined not to allow the terrorists direct access to anyone outside the embassy, and so were unable to agree to this demand. Eventually, Salim agreed to the message being sent via diplomatic channels, and it was sent that evening. The text of the message was as follows:

---

[9]UK Home Office, Siege of the Iranian embassy – "Official History"

This should reach Iran from all of the hostages at 16 Princes Gate, dictated by the Second Secretary, Iranian embassy.

In order that world imperialism, meaning the US and all its supporters, do not benefit from the act of holding these hostages by a number of our Iranian/Arab brothers attached to the martyr group of Muhieddin al Nassir, and lest they have a chance to take another step against weak nations. Therefore all of us who have signed this letter wish to represent our request to the Revolutionary Council and Minister of Foreign Affairs of Iran as follows, hoping that they will immediately investigate our request and announce a positive result.

1. We wish them to investigate and take necessary action regarding the requests of our brothers, the members of the Group of the Martyr Muhieddin an Nassir.

2. The request of our brothers is particularly to stress the point of our disagreement over the basic nature of independence, which is both lawful and reasonable, and is definitely worthy of investigation.

3. Not only have we no hostility towards them but they have been very fair in the majority of affairs and we are well aware of their humanitarian attitude.

4. In the name of Mighty God, in whom we all believe, in order to achieve this goal we will do our best and in our efforts we expect speedy cooperation and assistance from the officials of our beloved government.

From all the hostages and dictated by Mr Naghizadeh, Second Secretary of the Iranian embassy, London.

Tensions rose at 13:17, when LBC Radio broadcast a report that the terrorists had threatened to kill two hostages every two hours. The government complained to LBC Radio, pointing out that the report was wrong, and that it could lead to deaths among the hostages. LBC broadcast a retraction, which helped to ease tension within the embassy.

The 14:00 deadline passed without any issues. At 14:30 Salim said it would be extended to 16:30 if the telephone and telex lines were reconnected, but once again the police refused. Salim told the hostages that he was changing his demands. He now wanted Arab ambassadors to negotiate safe passage out of the country for the terrorists. He wanted transport to Heathrow Airport for the terrorists and hostages, with a Red Crescent representative to ensure safe transit. The mood among the hostages shot up, as they thought the police had agreed to these new demands. Their mood slumped again as they realised they were mistaken.

At 15:00, LBC broadcast a report that the British embassy in Tehran had been occupied. This wasn't true, but it angered the terrorists and provoked fighting between the pro- and anti-Khomeini protestors in Hyde Park. The police tried to separate the two sides, and one policeman suffered a broken leg in the ensuing melee.

At 15:08 Salim asked for twenty-five hamburgers, and thirty minutes later gave a fifteen-minute deadline for their arrival. Trays of food, including the hamburgers, were sent into the embassy shortly afterward. Once again, PC Lock refused to eat.

Salim gave new demands to the police at 16:45, stating that they were final. If they were not fulfilled by 19:00, all of the hostages would be killed. These new demands were basically those that he had told the hostages earlier that afternoon. A coach with curtained windows was to take the hostages and terrorists to a waiting aircraft, which was to have a mainly female crew. The ambassadors of Iraq, Algeria, and Jordan were to be waiting at the airport, where the non-Iranian hostages would be released. The aircraft was to take the terrorists and the Iranian hostages to the Middle East.

This was the first indication that the terrorists were now primarily concerned with safe passage out of the country. It wasn't clear if the demand for the release of Iranian prisoners had been dropped. Citing a need to consider the new demands, the police negotiated an extension of the deadline to 20:00.

A press conference was held at 18:15. Metropolitan Police Commissioner Sir David McNee appealed to the terrorists to remain calm and read out the list of demands, but did not mention the Arab ambassadors. This demand was particularly difficult for the British government, who were concerned that the ambassadors might have conflicting objectives. Unfortunately, the terrorists focused on this demand, and the government were unable to grant it. The British were determined not to allow the terrorists safe passage out of the country, and none of the ambassadors were willing to become involved unless they could offer such a guarantee. In fact, the British government couldn't allow the terrorists to leave. The UK is a signatory to the Convention on the Prevention and Punishment of Crimes against Internationally Protected Persons, including Diplomatic Agents.

Under the terms of the Convention, the UK had a duty to ensure the terrorists were available for prosecution or extradition. The Convention further obliged the UK to submit the case to the justice system for trial. Interestingly, at the time of the siege, Iran (also a signatory to the Convention), was in breach of the same obligation. Iranian students had taken over the American embassy in Tehran, and were still holding American diplomats hostage at the time of the siege. The United States had filed a case with the International Court of Justice, claiming that Iran had failed in its duty to arrest and prosecute the people holding their diplomats hostage.

The 20:00 deadline passed without incident, and a little after 21:00, PC Lock suggested that he could try talking to his colleagues. Salim agreed, and escorted him to a first-floor window. At 21:34, Lock leaned out, shouted his name and asked if anyone was there. One policeman came forward, and they conducted a shouted conversation.

PC Lock said that the situation was getting worse due to the delays. He said that the terrorists wanted an open telephone line and a coach to Heathrow. He added that the terrorists were edgy and did not trust the police. They had threatened to throw the field telephone out of the building, but had been persuaded to keep it since it was their only means of communication. A new deadline was set, of 08:00 on the 2nd of May.

At 22:25, PC Lock appeared at the window (which soon gained the nickname "talking window") with Sim Harris. The terrorists wanted to see one of Harris' BBC colleagues within an hour. Suspecting that the police were wasting time, Harris shouted down some direct telephone numbers. After a meal, during which Lock had only a glass of water and a biscuit, contact was made once again at about 00:45. The police said that no one from the BBC was available. Harris didn't believe them. The siege was a huge news story, and the BBC were being offered a scoop. Any news reporter would jump at the chance. PC Lock reported that morale was good and that the hostages were being treated well. The police took this as an encouraging sign, hoping that it was an indication of increasing empathy between hostages and terrorists. The 08:00 deadline was repeated, this time with a request that the police contact the terrorists at that time.

During the day, the UN Secretary General, Kurt Waldheim, had condemned the hostage takers, calling for restraint and safe release of the hostages. Iran and Iraq swapped insults. The Iraqi news agency in Beirut expressed sympathy for the hostage-taking and said it was time to "aim a knock-out blow at the Persian racists". The Iranians, in return, said that the Iraqi regime was an agent of American imperialism and Zionism. A spokesman for the Iranian Foreign Ministry said that he had heard that there were plans to occupy the British embassy in Tehran. He warned against it, urging people to keep calm. The British ambassador to Iran had already closed the embassy for the day after receiving a bomb threat by telephone. Tehran radio, responding to mistaken reports that the terrorists were demanding the release of the hostages in the American embassy in Tehran, claimed that the operation had been organised by the CIA and British Intelligence.

The SAS

"Gentlemen, the boy Stirling is mad. Quite, quite mad. But in war, there is a place for mad people."

— Field Marshal Montgomery on David Stirling, the founder of the SAS

The SAS trace their origins to the North African desert in World War II, where a Guards Colonel named David Stirling had an idea for a new type of unit. Knowing that his idea would be quietly dropped in the normal chain of command, Stirling decided to go straight to the top. Despite having a broken leg and needing crutches, he broke into the headquarters in Cairo. He intended to present his idea to the Commander in Chief, General Claude Auchinleck. Instead, he found General Ritchie, the deputy commander. Ritchie listened to Stirling's plan and convinced Auchinleck to allow him to form a new special forces unit.

The new unit was named "L Detachment, Special Air Service Brigade" in an attempt to disguise its true size and purpose. Unlike regular army units, L Detachment was organised into groups of four men, with no formal leader. It placed a great deal of emphasis on self-discipline rather than externally imposed discipline. Its first operation, a parachute drop in November 1941, was a disaster, with two-thirds of the unit captured, wounded, or killed. Stirling learned from the mistakes made, and the next mission was a great success, destroying sixty aircraft on three airfields with no losses. L Detachment continued to achieve remarkable results, and was renamed 1st SAS in September 1942. By then it consisted of six squadrons (four British, one Free French, one Greek), and an attached "folboat" section, which used folding canoes for infiltration by sea.

The SAS later operated in Sicily, Italy, and northwestern Europe, but like many other units that were created during the war, it was disbanded in October 1945. A Territorial Army unit (21st SAS Regiment) was created in 1947 as a deep-penetration commando unit. In 1952, 22nd SAS Regiment (22 SAS) was formed as a full-time unit in the regular army. 22 SAS is the smallest regiment in the British army, but it has proved itself to be flexible and efficient, producing results out of proportion to its size. Over the years, the regiment has assumed new responsibilities, including that of hostage rescue.

In the late 1960s and early 1970s, the SAS provided bodyguard training to friendly heads of state, and in a few select cases, SAS troopers were seconded as bodyguards. After the 1972 Munich massacre, where eleven Israeli Olympic athletes were killed, several Western governments decided to form dedicated hostage-rescue and anti-terrorist units. In Britain, this role was given to 22 SAS. The existing bodyguard training program formed the basis of the new Counter-Revolutionary Warfare (CRW) wing, also known as the Special Projects (SP) Team. The CRW studies terrorist methods and tactics. It develops and practices counter-terrorism and hostage-rescue techniques. An integral Operations Research Unit develops specialised equipment for counter-terrorist work.

The SAS already had expertise in combating revolutionary and guerrilla forces, but this had previously taken place abroad, not in the

UK. This new role was much more likely to involve operations in the UK, and was focused on smaller-scale operations. The CRW wing trained to carry out surveillance and break sieges in buildings, trains, and aircraft, with a heavy emphasis on close-quarter fighting. A "Close Quarter Battle House" (colloquially known as the "Killing House") had been established as part of the bodyguard training program. With the advent of the CRW wing, the Killing House was adapted for the new mission of rescuing hostages.

The SAS formed close relationships with similar units in other countries, such as GSG-9 in West Germany and GIGN in France. Cross-training and joint exercises were often conducted with foreign units. Sharing of intelligence and techniques was also common.

Initially, the CRW wing had around twenty men, and it was first deployed in January 1975. An Iranian, armed with a toy pistol and imitation dynamite, seized a British Airways aeroplane en route from Manchester to London Heathrow. The hijacker allowed the passengers to leave, in return for a promise that the aircraft would fly on to Paris. In fact, the pilot flew the aircraft to Stansted. The hijacker was arrested peacefully and the SAS were stood down.

In December of the same year, four IRA terrorists took two hostages in a flat on Balcombe Street, London. Knowing that the terrorists had a radio, the police arranged for the BBC news to announce that an SAS team was standing by to carry out an assault if needed. The IRA had encountered the regiment in Northern Ireland. IRA members had a great deal of respect for, and some fear of, the SAS. After a six-day siege, the terrorists surrendered. Once again, the SAS were stood down.

Some issues around command and control became apparent during the Balcombe Street siege, but a compromise solution was reached for future use. In purely criminal cases, the police would retain full control. If the issue was of a political nature (e.g., the hostage-takers were attempting to coerce the British, or any other government), then negotiations and operations would be directed by COBR.

The police retain tactical control of the scene until control is passed to the MOD. The SAS role is one of Military Aid to the Civil Power (MACP). MACP is defined as "the provision of military assistance to the Civil Power in the maintenance of law, order, and public safety, using specialist capabilities or equipment, in situations beyond the capacity of the Civil Power". Rules of engagement for the SAS are worked out before control is passed to the MOD, and once the operation is concluded, control is passed back to the police. The police conduct a criminal investigation to determine whether or not the rules of engagement were followed. The soldiers involved can face charges of murder if the police find evidence that excessive force was used.

Members of the CRW wing advised Dutch forces prior to a rescue mission against terrorists that had hijacked a train in May 1977. Their role in this mission was purely advisory. Although they were present at the assault, they did not take an active part.

In October 1977, four terrorists hijacked Lufthansa flight 181 and took the crew and passengers hostage. The aircraft was moved around, eventually landing in Mogadishu, Somalia. Two SAS men, Major Alistair Morrison and Sergeant Barry Davies, were dispatched to help the West German hostage-rescue unit, GSG9. They carried with them a crate of stun grenades, newly developed by the Operations Research Unit.

Major Morrison and Sergeant Davies were able to help negotiate with the Somali authorities, and helped with planning and conducting the assault. Two terrorists were killed, and the other two were wounded, one of whom died a few hours later. All of the hostages were rescued, with four hostages and one GSG-9 commando sustaining minor injuries. The operation was a stunning success.

Major Morrison and Sergeant Davies were personally thanked in Bonn by the West German Chancellor, Helmut Schmidt. Major Morrison was awarded the Order of the British Empire (OBE)[10], and Sergeant Davies the British Empire Medal (BEM)[11]. Mogadishu proved the worth of an effective hostage-rescue unit. The British government allocated extra funding to the SAS, leading to an expansion of the CRW wing. Each of the four sabre squadrons began to rotate through CRW duty in six-month cycles. At the time of the Iranian embassy siege, B squadron had just taken over as the on-duty CRW squadron.

---

[10]10. TNA: WO 373/177/14
[11]11. TNA: WO/373/177/79

2nd May 1980: Day 3

Blue Team moved from Regent's Park Barracks to the Doctor's House in nondescript white hire vans, arriving at around 03:30. By this time, Red Team had been on standby for twenty-four hours. Blue Team changed into assault kit and prepared their weapons. Once they had been briefed by the Red Team commander, they settled in and took over the standby role. New intelligence had been acquired, and the assault plan had been significantly improved from the hurriedly-prepared IA plan. Red Team moved to Regent's Park Barracks while Blue Team familiarised themselves with potential entry points that had been identified on the roof.

The SAS had kept a low profile, and there was no sign that any of them had been recognised as soldiers by the media. Wearing civilian clothes, and with long hair, they weren't obviously soldiers. Still, that morning's Guardian newspaper had an article on page two headlined "Pagoda, the SAS unit waiting in the wings". The article discussed how police would request help from the SAS via COBR, and noted that the SAS had not previously been employed to rescue hostages in Britain.

In Iran, Tehran Radio reported that the pro-Khomeini demonstrators in Hyde Park were being badly treated and denied food and blankets, despite cold weather. The Iranian president asked the British ambassador, Sir John Graham, about this. Sir Graham checked with London, and was told that demonstrators were being contained within a cordon. They were free to leave the cordon, but once they left, they were not allowed back in. The ambassador also reported that things were quiet in Tehran, though threats had been made against the embassy. Later that day, it was decided that embassy staffing levels would be reduced to the bare minimum.

The police hope that the forced closeness would foster empathy towards the hostages on the part of the terrorists seemed to be misplaced. A listening device picked up a woman screaming and saying "don't drag me". At 08:10 Salim put the phone down, saying "Now we are going to kill the hostages. We have given you enough time since Wednesday and you didn't do anything"[12]. It wasn't all bad news, though. Salim had confirmed that they were no longer demanding the release of prisoners in Iran. Now they simply wanted an aeroplane to fly them out of the country.

Salim decided that the British authorities would not take their demands seriously unless they killed a hostage. PC Lock managed to convince Salim to allow him to talk to the police on behalf of the terrorists. Dr Abdul Ezzati, a diplomat who had annoyed the terrorists, was chosen and taken to the talking window with Lock and Karkouti. On Salim's instructions, Lock shouted down that a hostage was going to be killed unless the telephone and telex lines were re-connected. This was refused, and Ezzati, believing he was about to be killed, collapsed to the floor, convulsing. He was taken back to room nine. The other hostages, knowing that he had a heart condition and suspecting a minor heart attack, asked for his release, but the terrorists refused.

---

[12]UK Home Office, Siege of the Iranian embassy – "Official History"

Salim, still at the window, told the police that Harris had asked for a BBC man to come to the embassy. The police quickly agreed, hoping that it would help to reduce the tension. They knew that several BBC executives had organised a shift system at Television House, so that one was always available for a request such as this. They were soon able to tell Salim that Tony Crabb was on his way. Crabb was a friend of Harris and the Managing Editor of BBC TV News. Pleased, Salim went back and collected Afrouz, Harris, Lock, and Karkouti, taking them down to the ground floor.

Crabb arrived a little after 09:00, and after a quick police briefing, went forward with a negotiator to the front of the embassy. The negotiator called out for Salim. Harris immediately recognised Crabb, and told Salim who he was. Salim was pleased, but warned Harris not to say anything about the terrorists or where they kept the hostages. Salim opened the window and told Harris to ask why the police were not cooperating. Harris went to the window and told Crabb, "You've got to get it over to the Government how the police are acting. They've cut off the phones and telex so the Iranians can't communicate. There were two statements yesterday about mediation"[13].

Crabb asked what the mediation proposal was. Salim, through Harris, said that he wanted the Algerian, Jordanian, and Iraqi ambassadors, with a representative of the Red Cross, to mediate. When they got to the airport, the non-Iranian hostages would be left behind. The ambassadors would travel in the aeroplane with the terrorists and the Iranian hostages. Harris added that he believed the terrorists were sincere. The tension had built to a high level, and the terrorists wanted to calm things down. He said that the hostages had formed "very good relationships with our captors but the police are determined to upset things by opening doubts"[14]. Sounds akin to

---

[13]UK Home Office, Siege of the Iranian embassy – "Official History"
[14]UK Home Office, Siege of the Iranian embassy – "Official History"

drilling had been heard during the night, and this worried the terrorists. Afrouz came to the window and asked for the telephone and telex lines to be re-connected so that he could contact his Government in Tehran. "They are our brothers" he said. "We are all Muslims".

This was the first indication to the British authorities that the terrorists wanted the Arab ambassadors to leave the country with them. The British government had already decided that the terrorists would not be permitted to leave the country, but warned the ambassadors that a request had been made for them to mediate. The authorities took this new demand to indicate a shift in priorities among the terrorists. They now seemed to be more concerned with saving their own lives than furthering their cause. This was seen as a positive change, since they were more likely to negotiate and eventually give themselves up.

Once the window had been closed, the police negotiators contacted Salim to talk about food. Salim wanted proof that their demands were being taken seriously, and asked again for the telephone to be reconnected. The interpreter spoke to Salim in Farsi about releasing someone, suggesting either a British or female hostage. Salim was determined not to release anyone until they got to the airport, saying "Our peaceful attitude is diminishing. We want this plan by five or six o'clock"[15]. He also wanted food to be delivered between 12:00 and 13:00, including some canned drinks. The police agreed, and organised lunch from a nearby Persian restaurant, which was delivered to the embassy's front door. Inside the embassy, the arrival of food allowed everyone to calm down a little. Lock, still wary of eating too much, only ate some cheese and biscuits. Harris consoled himself that at least Crabb would be able to assure his wife, Helen, that he was well.

---

[15]UK Home Office, Siege of the Iranian embassy – "Official History"

After lunch, Karkouti, Harris, Lock, and Faruqi talked to Salim, while Faisal watched over them. Harris counselled patience, saying that many meetings would be required to get what the terrorists wanted. While the others talked, Karkouti listened to a radio, with the volume turned low. Hearing an LBC report that two Arabs had been executed in Iran for organising anti-Khomeini demonstrations, he signalled Faruqi to keep the conversation going. Faruqi talked of the publicity that the siege would be generating across the world. He told Salim that if it became violent, the group would lose everything they had gained. Lock suggested that the terrorists should give themselves up. He emphasised that the terrorists would be treated with decency, that they would not be tortured or harmed. Salim got angry, shouting that giving up would be surrender, and moved the men back into room nine. The siege would continue.

Back in room nine, Lavasani had come to a decision. He told the others that if the terrorists wanted a victim, he would volunteer. His only close family were his parents, so he reasoned he had less to lose. After writing out a will, he said goodbye to the other hostages and knelt to pray. He was preparing for martyrdom.

That afternoon, the Home Secretary, William Whitelaw, met with the Prime Minister, Margaret Thatcher, to discuss how the siege might end[16]. They were hopeful that the terrorists would eventually surrender and release the hostages unharmed. It had already been agreed on the first day of the siege that an assault would be mounted if any hostages were killed. Plans needed to be agreed upon for other contingencies, however.

One contingency was that the terrorists might be persuaded to release the hostages, but still demand safe passage out of the country. Granting safe passage in such a case would mean no loss of life. It would avoid further terrorist attacks aimed at releasing the terrorists if they were imprisoned in the UK. On the other hand, strong

---

[16] Margaret Thatcher Foundation archive, document ID 128193

criticism could be expected from the international community, and the UK would appear to be weak in the face of terrorism. Whitelaw recommended that an assault should be carried out in this case. He had discussed this with ministers at the Foreign and Commonwealth Office, who shared his view. Mrs Thatcher agreed. Consequently, the only way for the siege to end peacefully was for the terrorists to give themselves up without harming any hostages. Unbeknownst to Whitelaw or Thatcher, Salim had angrily rejected this possibility.

The home secretary agreed to keep the prime minister appraised of developments, and to consult with her over major decisions if there was time to do so. In an emergency, the home secretary was authorised to order whatever action he felt necessary. In the event of an assault, the SAS would be allowed to make their own decisions about how best to proceed. The prime minister agreed to all this, but pointed out that the recent American failure to rescue hostages in Tehran made it especially important that any assault must succeed.

Negotiations that afternoon were relaxed. Advice was given about Ezzati's heart condition. The terrorists requested, and received, a pair of trousers for one of the hostages. The terrorists confirmed that they wanted the Arab ambassadors to come to the embassy rather than the airport. The vaguely-worded deadline of "five or six o'clock" passed without trouble, although Salim did make it clear that they had considered the possibility of an assault by the British. He warned the police that "we can kill the hostages no matter how quick you think you are". He asked for the telex line to be restored once again, but he was not prepared to release any hostages in exchange. The police were not prepared to reconnect the lines, especially not without a hostage's release in return.

The women were being kept separate from the men; they were guarded by Ali in the small cypher room (room 9A). The women were starting to develop a rapport with Ali, and talked to him about his family and his homeland. They also told him that they had heard noises from the adjoining building. Salim once again told Lock to investigate, and he made a show of doing so, but was determined not to find anything. While Lock was doing this, Harris quietly told one of the women to stop drawing attention to the noises, saying that the police were trying to listen in on what was happening.

By 23:00, Salim was getting angry at the lack of progress, and the hostages worried that the terrorists were going to start shooting. At 23:30, a BBC report stated that the terrorists wanted Arab ambassadors to negotiate with the Iranian government. The error increased Salim's anger. The police quickly sent a carton of two hundred cigarettes into the embassy, which helped to calm Salim down.

Meanwhile, in Hyde Park, the pro-Khomeini demonstrators had left. The police tactic of allowing them to leave the cordon but not return had reduced their numbers. Earlier in the day, the Iranian Consul-General had told them that the Iranian government had issued instructions that they were to leave, and they did as they were told. The demonstrators' chants had carried to the embassy, so their removal helped reduce tension significantly.

Elsewhere, the British government had been holding discussions with the Arab ambassadors requested by the terrorists. There was a degree of ambiguity over which ones would be acceptable. Originally, they had asked for the Iraqi, Jordanian, and Algerian ambassadors, but the Syrian and Libyan ambassadors had also been mentioned. Negotiators felt the Kuwaiti and Bahraini ambassadors might also be acceptable.

The British refused to consider the Libyan ambassador, and the others wanted to consult with their governments before they would commit to anything. Jordan was a long-standing ally of Britain, and the ambassador was initially helpful. That changed when he received instructions from Amman. Jordan had a long-standing policy of never talking to, or negotiating with, terrorists. The Jordanian government felt that this policy would be undermined if their ambassador acted as a mediator.

The other ambassadors refused to help once it became clear that the British would not allow the terrorists to go free under any circumstances. The British policy meant that they would have no room to negotiate. The Iraqi ambassador was a notable exception. He was willing to help, as long as he could talk personally to the terrorists. The British refused, saying that it would undermine the work of the police negotiators. By this time, it was already clear that Iraq had a hand in the takeover of the embassy, so Iraq's offer of help must have been viewed with a great deal of suspicion.

3rd May 1980: Day 4

The previous day, the hostages had found some large floor cushions, and so they got a much better night's sleep. They hadn't been able to wash or change clothes for several days, and it was starting to affect morale. PC Lock, who hadn't removed his tunic or overcoat since the siege began, worried that he was starting to smell. Nonetheless, when anyone suggested that he should take them off, he refused, saying that he was still on duty. While the Iranians conducted morning prayers, Sim Harris volunteered to unblock a toilet. He took the opportunity to get a wash, making himself feel rather more human.

By now, the siege had been going on for long enough that things felt almost normal. The atmosphere of fear had been largely replaced with one of boredom. To pass the time, the hostages read magazines, official letters, and memos. Most of them were only of interest because there was nothing better to read, although there were a few interesting pieces among all the tedium. Ahmed Dadgar read a copy of Day of the Jackal that he had found, and promised to pass it on once he had finished. Unfortunately for the others, he was a slow reader.

The Iranian government had made it clear that they would not accept any involvement by the Iraqis. The Iraqi ambassador, on the other hand, was very keen to help. The British had no intention of allowing the Iraqi ambassador to get involved, but COBR was concerned that the terrorists might react badly if they realised this. The police had picked up on the improved atmosphere in the embassy, and were fairly optimistic that a peaceful outcome would be reached.

That optimism was shattered as early as 09:10. Salim had been listening to Tehran Radio, which said that any Arab ambassadors who agreed to mediate would be negotiating with the Iranian government, not the British. Despite knowing that Tehran Radio could not be trusted, this made him angry. Talking to the negotiators via the field telephone, he refused breakfast, and ignored the demand for ambassadors. Instead he concentrated on the BBC's failure to broadcast the message that had been given to Tony Crabb the previous day. Finally, he said that he would not talk on the telephone, and insisted on face to face negotiations. Then he hung up.

The atmosphere in room nine changed abruptly at 11:30, when Salim barged in. He demanded to know why the BBC had not broadcast the group's message. Harris suggested that the government might have issued a D notice (an official request not to broadcast). This didn't please Salim, who dictated a message to Lock. Then he ordered Lock, Afrouz, and Karkouti to the talking window.

PC Lock appeared at the window at 12:13. He told the officer on the ground that he'd written down what the terrorists had told him to say, and then read from his notebook. It started with an appeal not to force the terrorists to take actions that they very much wanted to avoid, such as killing a hostage. It repeated the request for the ambassadors, because they represented a guarantee of safety for both the terrorists and the hostages. They wanted the previous day's interview with Tony Crabb to be broadcast. In an increasingly hysterical tone, the final demand was for Crabb. If he was not produced at once, a hostage would be killed.

Next, Karkouti spoke for the hostages. He said that morale was deteriorating, and blamed the delaying tactics of the police[17]:

> *"I believe that tension is being built on us. They suspect that you have invoked a D notice on the interview yesterday. They are intelligent and educated men and are aware of this procedure. As far as they are concerned, they have completed their expedition and now wish to leave but it has been delayed by your response to their request. The only sufferers will be the hostages".*

He also said that no one in the embassy cared about the "inhuman" Iranian government response, "so we are seeking the humanity of the British because it seems it is the only way out". The police noted the use of "us" and "we" by Karkouti. They hoped that this was an indication of bonds forming between terrorists and hostages. Such bonds would make it harder for the terrorists to kill the hostages, making a peaceful conclusion more likely.

Afrouz then came to the window. Like Karkouti, his language suggested a bond with the terrorists[18].

> *"Our relationship with those around us is not of oppressor and oppressed. Whatever I am telling is not at gunpoint. I am saying this willingly. They have been treating us very nicely and I shall never forget their kindness. As diplomats our problem is that of the British Government. We have no TV or telephone. Please allow the newscaster [Crabb] to pay us a visit so that we can be heard. But the group and the hostages, our aim is to finalise the affair peacefully".*

Salim gave the police one hour to produce Crabb. The police warned that it would be difficult to get him so quickly. However, they assured Salim that if no harm was done to the hostages, no action would be taken to force their release. They suggested that the

---

[17]UK Home Office, Siege of the Iranian embassy – "Official History"
[18]UK Home Office, Siege of the Iranian embassy – "Official History"

terrorists could hold a press conference on the embassy steps, but Salim rejected the idea.

When Crabb did not arrive within an hour, tension in the embassy increased dramatically. Ali Aghar Tabatabai, who spent most of the siege in good spirits, wept. Karkouti complained of sharp pains in his stomach. Noting the similarity to Cramer's symptoms, Harris wondered if the police were tampering with the food that was sent in. Lock assured him that they wouldn't do that.

Much to everyone's relief, at 15:30 Crabb arrived in an unmarked police car. An angry Harris went to the talking window, wanting to know why the statement hadn't been broadcast. A confused Crabb said that he didn't realise it was intended for broadcast, and pointed out that he didn't make those decisions. Harris, still angry, retorted that he was senior enough to have some influence, should he choose to exercise it.

Salim asked Crabb to take down a statement dictated by Karkouti, and Harris reiterated that the hostages' lives were at stake. Crabb took the statement, which was also immediately forwarded to COBR.[19]

> 1. We swear to God and to the British people and Government that no danger whatsoever would be inflicted on the British and non-Iranian hostages as well as the Iranian hostages if the British Government and the British police don't kid the group and don't subject the life of the hostages and the group to any danger, and if things work to the contradictory direction everyone in this building will be harmed.

> 2. We demand the three ambassadors, Algerian, Jordanian, and Iraqi and a representative of the Red Cross to start their jobs in negotiating between us and the British Government to secure the safety of the hostages as well as the group's members and to terminate the whole operation peacefully. If any of the three ambassadors is not available they could be substituted by, first, the Libyan, or the Syrian, or the Kuwaiti ambassador.

---

[19] UK Home Office, Siege of the Iranian embassy – "Official History"

3. The reason for us to come to Britain to carry out this operation is because of the pressure and oppression which is being practiced by the Iranian Government in Arabistan and to convey our voice through the outside world to your country. Once again we apologise to the people and Government for this inconvenience.

Karkouti finished by saying that there would be a "positive response"[20] if the statement was broadcast. Once Karkouti had finished, Afrouz appeared at the window and threw out two pieces of paper, saying that they were a genuine message from the hostages. The message was headed "For the attention of His Excellency Mr Bani Sadr, the President of the Islamic Republic of Iran". The message displayed some sympathy for the terrorists' cause, and sought a peaceful conclusion. This directly contradicted Ghotbzadeh's claim that the hostages would consider it an honour and a privilege to die as martyrs. The message read:

In order to put an end to the false and mischievous propaganda being mounted by Imperialist and pro-Imperialist forces, we wish to clarify the situation as follows:

The group which is presently occupying the premises of the embassy of the Islamic Republic in London has stated that they belong to the Group of Mohedin Al-Nasser.

They state and assure us that they are struggling for their legitimate rights as 'Arab - IRANIANS' and they are not against Islam. They do not want to break away from Iran and their demand is only for self-rule within the Islamic Republic of Iran.

They have also assured us that they are patriotic IRANIANS, and they are not working for any Imperialist or anti-Islamic group.

From what we have known of them and seen of them during this time, we believe that they are genuine, young, militant people devoted to their cause. They have also treated all those confined in this embassy in a pleasant and humane manner.

---

[20]UK Home Office, Siege of the Iranian embassy – "Official History"

This makes us believe that the present situation can be resolved peacefully and honourably for all the people concerned.

The group also feels that they have made their grievances known to the people concerned, and the only problem which needs to be resolved is to work out a formula so that the present situation can be ended peacefully.

This seems to be possible only through the good offices of some Arab ambassadors whom the group can trust and who can give good counsel to the group. We fully support the bringing in of such good offices and told the authorities accordingly.

The hostages in the embassy of the Islamic Republic of Iran.

Back inside, Salim picked up the field telephone to discuss the "positive response" that had been promised in return for broadcasting the statement. Salim offered to free one hostage in return for the broadcast, but the negotiator held out for more. After some discussion, Salim agreed to release two hostages.

After some discussion, the terrorists decided that the two hostages to be freed would be Mrs Hiyech Sanei Kanji and Ali Guil Ghanzafar. As noted earlier, Mrs Kanji was pregnant, although this had been hidden from the terrorists earlier during the siege. Ghanzafar was chosen because he snored loudly, and he constantly annoyed the terrorists.

Multiple broadcast organisations were asked to read the statement on air by 21:00. Particular attention was paid to the BBC World Service, because it was believed that the terrorists were listening to that station.

There were problems within the embassy. At 19:00, Tehran Radio claimed that British police were planning to storm the embassy, and that they were only waiting for permission from the Iranian government. PC Lock assured Salim that this was not true. Not only did that go against British policy, he said, they wouldn't ask another government for permission.

An angry Salim went to the field telephone, with Karkouti and Lock, escorted by other terrorists. He demanded to know why the statement had not been broadcast. The police said that the two hostages had to be released first. Salim yelled into the phone, then stormed off. Lock was convinced it was finally going to end, violently. Harris managed to persuade Salim to allow him to talk to the police. He wanted to make sure there were no more mistakes. He was assured that the full statement would be read on BBC Radio 1, Radio 2, and the World Service.

Karkouti asked Salim to release a hostage as a goodwill gesture. Mrs Kanji was taken downstairs. Tensions were running high; the other hostages wondered if she was going to be killed. At 20:15, she walked out of the door. The terrorists had given her a message for the police: If the statement was broadcast by 21:00 another hostage would be released. If not, two hostages would be killed.

The statement was broadcast, in full, on LBC, BBC Radio, and BBC TV. The BBC World Service only broadcast a summary, not the full statement. The police waited for two dead bodies to appear, but they never did. At 21:20, to everyone's surprise and relief, Ali Guil Ghanzafar walked out of the embassy door. The terrorists had been listening to Radio 2. The full statement had been broadcast at 20:52, and they were very happy. So were the hostages. The World Service were asked to read the statement in full, and this was done at 21:28. It was repeated on Radio 4 at 22:00. Salim was slightly annoyed that this broadcast described Ghanzafar as Iranian, but the negotiator agreed to have the mistake rectified, and offered to send in food.

Both Mrs Kanji and Ghanzafar were taken to hospital at Hendon. Doctors gave them a check-up, and police debriefed them. Mrs Kanji was "extremely helpful"[21], but Ghanzafar was of little help. He had told Salim that he would say nothing to the police, and he kept his word.

---

[21]TNA: PREM 19/1137

At this point, the terrorists and hostages were all in good spirits. Negotiations seemed to be going well, and two hostages had been released that day. The food arrived (Persian for the Iranians, English for the British, as requested), and everyone sat down to eat. Karkouti ate very little. He still wasn't feeling well. The terrorists, knowing that he'd complained of stomach pains earlier, wanted to release him next. Karkouti wanted to stay. As the only fluent speaker of both English and Arabic, he was likely to be needed as a translator. He had also managed to calm Salim down more than once, a very useful talent.

The SAS decided to take advantage of the good mood within the embassy and the terrorists' distraction. At 23:00 a team climbed up onto the roof of the Doctor's House. They carefully moved across to the embassy roof to do a close reconnaissance. Suddenly there was a loud crack. The SAS froze, thinking it was a pistol shot. In fact, one of the men had broken a roof tile. There was no discernible reaction from inside the embassy so, after giving the watching snipers a thumbs-up, they continued.

On the embassy roof, the team found a skylight over a small bathroom. It was locked, but careful work with a knife allowed them to remove the lead holding a large pane of glass in place, and they were able to lift the glass away. At this point, they had a covert means of entry into the building. It wasn't necessarily a good or useful entry point, since there was no way to know if the interior door was barricaded on the other side. Nonetheless, it was another nugget of information to be considered when planning the potential assault.

Before returning to the Doctor's House, the team secured abseil ropes to chimney breasts. In the event of an assault, abseil teams could use these ropes to descend to the second-floor balcony and gain entry via the windows. Having the ropes already in position would save valuable time.

Meanwhile, at Regent's Park Barracks, contingency plans were being made in case the terrorists were allowed to leave the embassy in a coach. As well as planning and rehearsing an assault on the embassy, the SAS planned and rehearsed an attack on a coach. SAS soldiers, because they sometimes do undercover work, typically have longer hair than other soldiers, or policemen. Consequently, the man chosen to be the driver had to have a haircut in order to be passed off as a policeman. The coach assault would be carried out as an ambush at a prearranged spot, with snipers deployed to fire on targets if opportunities presented themselves.

During the evening, COBR discussed the difficult issue of intermediaries. The Chairman of the British Red Cross Society, Sir Evelyn Shuckburgh, said that the Red Cross was willing to relay messages, but nothing more. In particular, they were not prepared to become involved in any mediations or negotiations. Of the ambassadors whom the terrorists had named, the British would not accept the Iraqi or Libyan ambassadors. The Algerian and Jordanian ambassadors had received instructions not to get involved. This left the Kuwaiti and the Syrian. Of the two, the British much preferred the Kuwaiti, although they would agree to the Syrian as well if the Kuwaiti did not wish to act alone.

COBR decided that Douglas Hurd, Minister of State at the Foreign & Commonwealth Office, was to talk to the Kuwaiti the next day. Hurd knew the Kuwaiti ambassador well. He was to try and find out if he would be willing to act according to the British Government's instructions. Hurd was far from sure that the ambassador would agree to this, so the police were instructed to try and steer negotiations away from the ambassadors.

Like the terrorists and hostages inside the embassy, COBR had high hopes that the siege would be ended peacefully. The terrorists were getting a great deal of publicity for their cause, which appeared to be their main goal. Everyone knew that the siege was entering a difficult stage, but there was a feeling of optimism in the air.

The home secretary rang the prime minister just before midnight, to give her a summary of the day's events. She agreed with the stance that COBR had taken regarding the ambassadors. They were both hopeful that the terrorists would eventually agree to surrender, having secured a great deal of publicity for their cause. Mrs Thatcher congratulated Whitelaw on the work he had done, and Whitelaw said that the police had also done an excellent job[22].

---

[22]Margaret Thatcher Foundation archive, document ID 128194

4th May 1980: Day 5

Knowing that the ambassador issue was going to be a difficult one, a Home Office official summarised the relevant parts of the previous evening's COBR meeting into a set of guidance notes for the negotiators. These were sent to the police in the early hours of 4th May. As in COBR, the police knew that things weren't going to be easy, but they were optimistic: so much so that they granted a request from HRH Prince Andrew to visit Zulu Control.

Inside the embassy, PC Lock had his first wash since the siege began. Luckily, he managed to persuade the terrorist who accompanied him to allow him to wash alone. Had the terrorist stayed with Lock, he would almost certainly have discovered the policeman's revolver, with potentially disastrous results. The gamble paid off, and being clean greatly improved Lock's spirits. Given his central role in maintaining the morale of the hostages, this was very helpful.

Salim was also in a good mood, pleased that Arabistan's cause had been broadcast world-wide. He decided that the hostages would be allowed to wash. Ahmed Dadgar found his razor, and was able to shave off his five-day beard. Both he and the terrorists splashed on aftershave. Toothpaste was found and shared among both hostages and terrorists. The improvement in cleanliness helped improve everyone's mood. The atmosphere improved even more when the BBC reported that some Arab ambassadors were willing to cooperate.

The police made a routine call at 10:00. They had nothing to offer, but wanted to keep the atmosphere friendly and relaxed. Inside, the mood slowly changed to one of boredom. The hostages searched for something to read, and Salim lectured them on the plight of his people, how the Group of the Martyr were fighting for the Arabistan People's Political Organisation (APPO). This did little to alleviate the boredom, since the hostages had heard it all before. Moreover, none of them wanted to die for Salim's cause.

Faruqi, Harris, Karkouti, and PC Lock brought the subject around to surrender. They emphasised that the group's message had been broadcast, not just in the UK, but world-wide. This was an excellent success, they argued, and so it would be better to end now, while the group was ahead.

Karkouti suggested a press conference inside the embassy, with cameramen and reporters. The hostages could be released as soon as the conference was broadcast. Salim wasn't convinced. It's unlikely the police would have agreed, since the news reporters would have been potential hostages.

Salim did ask PC Lock about British law, what offences they had committed, and how long they would be likely to spend in prison. Lock replied that, outside the embassy, the only offence was illegal possession of a firearm. They would likely be sentenced to four years in prison, but would serve less time if they showed good behaviour. He didn't mention the various offenses that they had committed inside the embassy. The cumulative term for those was likely to be significant. Unfortunately, he did mention the possibility that the British government would deport them. Although Salim didn't much like the idea of time in a British gaol, the Iranian government was likely to hand down an even worse punishment.

Ghotbzadeh, the Iranian Foreign Minister, told a press conference that if Britain decided "for one reason or another that they are not able to cope with this problem, we are going to take things into our hands to resolve this as we see fit".

Salim spoke to the negotiators in the early afternoon, but there was little they could tell him. They were still awaiting the outcome of FCO discussions. They didn't want to tell him that the Iraqi was unacceptable until they had some good news to soften the blow. Good news was in short supply, so the best they could do was tell him that an ambassador had not been found, but attempts were ongoing.

The police didn't want an ambassador to talk directly to the terrorists any more than the government did. Dellow told a press conference that he wanted it to remain a police operation. He pointed out that international experience had shown that civilian intermediaries could be dangerous. The terrorists knew that the police had no real power to effect government policy. This meant that the negotiators could blame delays and problems on others. In this way, they were able to give the impression of wanting to help but being thwarted by others. This all helped to garner trust and build a rapport, which was essential if the siege was to be ended peacefully.

Around 13:30 Salim asked Harris if a programme would be made about the siege. Harris replied that news reporters would be very interested in making documentaries. Salim decided to give them something to film. Three of the terrorists, taking pens from the embassy's stationary cupboard, started writing anti-Iranian slogans on the walls. Afrouz was incensed when he saw a slogan proclaiming "Death to Khomeini". He started shouting at the hostages that they had to fight the terrorists. Faruqi tried to calm him down, but Lavasani got up and joined Afrouz. The other Iranians tried to calm Afrouz and Lavasani, but they were too angry. Hassan, on guard at the door, took a hand grenade from his pocket, yelling at them to shut up.

Three other terrorists ran to the room and brandished their weapons at the hostages, intimidating them temporarily. This didn't last, and when the shouting started up again, Salim headed to the room with Karkouti. Things were getting out of hand. Afrouz, Lavasani, and the terrorists were all shouting at each other. Suddenly, Lavasani charged at Faisal. Faisal forced him to the floor and cocked his submachine gun. Faisal was screaming and pointing his gun at Lavasani. Several Iranians tried to restrain Lavasani. Lock looked him in the eye and shouted at him to calm down. Karkouti sat in front of Lavasani, shielding him from Faisal. Eventually, Lavasani calmed down, and hugged Karkouti, kissing him on the cheeks.

Salim left, presumably to help keep the atmosphere calm, but Faisal kept taunting the Iranians. The other Iranians tried to keep Lavasani calm, but Faisal started writing slogans on the walls in the room. Lavasani shouted at him, struggling as others held him down. Faisal walked over to Lavasani, and told him, "If you want to die, we will kill you!" After telling the others that they were not to talk, he left the room. The hostages did as they were told, which meant that they were able to hear the terrorists arguing outside. Faisal wanted to make an example of Lavasani. After some time, Faisal came back in and told the hostages that they could talk in whispers, but the Iranians were to pray individually, in silence. The police's listening probes had picked up the argument, which worried the negotiators. They still had nothing to offer the terrorists.

Meanwhile, the FCO was talking to the ambassadors of Kuwait, Jordan, Algeria, and Syria. When they realised that their only role was to persuade the terrorists to surrender, they all refused. The wrong move could cause trouble with Iraq, Iran, or both. They had nothing to gain, but much to lose. Tensions were growing inside the embassy, and no one was willing to help secure the terrorists' surrender. The possibility of a peaceful end to the siege was diminishing rapidly.

The embassy was quiet and tense that afternoon. Even the terrorists barely spoke to each other. The police called Salim at 17:06 to tell him that the FCO had been unable to find an ambassador to talk to them, but they were still trying. Angry, Salim shouted that the hostages would be killed if an aircraft was not provided the next day. The negotiator stood firm. He told Salim that the terrorists would not get an aircraft, and that there would be trouble if any hostages were killed.

At 17:38 PC Lock appeared at the window, saying that the terrorists were complaining about drilling again, and that tensions were high. It was still quiet in the embassy. At 18:10 PC Lock was heard trying to explain why it was difficult to get ambassadors to talk to the terrorists, but Salim simply told him to shut up. In an effort to relieve tension, food was offered, but refused.

Karkouti's condition was deteriorating. He had complained of stomach pains the previous afternoon, which had become diarrhoea and a fever earlier that day. Now he started to complain of numbness in his limbs. Medicine was requested at 19:00, and delivered at 19:24. At 20:10, a negotiator called to enquire after the sick hostage, and was told that someone was coming out. A few minutes later, Karkouti stepped out of the embassy, holding his stomach.

He was taken to the Peel Centre Medical Unit, where a doctor examined him and said that he would not be able to withstand more than thirty minutes of questioning. Karkouti composed himself so quickly that he made the interviewing officer suspicious. He was keen to answer questions, but also asked to make a press statement on behalf of his "friends" (the terrorists), further fuelling suspicion.

Despite this initial mistrust, Karkouti provided the police and SAS with some very useful information. He was able to identify most of the hostages from photographs, and confirmed that there were six terrorists, armed with submachine guns and pistols. Each terrorist had at least one grenade, but the other weapons were swapped around. Salim had told him that they had got sufficient publicity, and he was now looking for a way out. Salim thought that the only way to ensure their safety was for the ambassadors to be present when they left the embassy. He had confessed to Karkouti that they were all tired. What they had expected to be a twenty-eight-hour operation was now in its fifth day. Karkouti said that he and PC Lock both thought that Salim was losing control over the other terrorists. He did not believe that the women or non-Iranians were in any real danger, though. The terrorists had repeatedly stated that they would not kill them.

At Regent's Park Barracks, it wasn't all work and no play. A couple of members of Blue Team recruited a clerk from the Royal Army Ordnance Corps onto the assault team. They told him that one of the team was ill, and they needed a replacement immediately. Despite having no SAS training, let alone training in hostage-rescue work, he agreed. The clerk became visibly more worried as he went through a pre-brief and then a full briefing from Lieutenant-Colonel Rose. He was finally told the truth — that it was just a prank — at the end of the briefing.

A little before 21:00, Salim took Harris and PC Lock away from the other hostages, to listen to the radio. The news report was the first the two hostages heard of Karkouti's release. They were instructed not to tell the others, though Salim himself told Morris a little later.

At 21:06, a negotiator called Salim to thank him for the release of Karkouti. Salim replied that he did not want thanks, or food, just a meeting with the ambassadors, "to find a peaceful solution to all this"[23]. The negotiator noted that he sounded depressed. At 22:12, Salim asked about the Iraqi and Algerian ambassadors. He was told

[23]UK Home Office, Siege of the Iranian embassy – "Official History"

that it was too late for anything to happen that day, but that high-level talks were ongoing.

The day ended with bad news. Reuters reported that Tehran Radio had broadcast another message from Ghotbzadeh. Once again, he seemed confident in the hostages' willingness to become martyrs[24]:

> You, the revolutionary members of the Iranian embassy in London. We admire your steadfastness and forbearance against the criminal actions of the Ba'athist Iraq as well as those of the agents of Imperialism and international Zionism. But we want you to know that in these critical moments in which you have been placed under heavy pressure by these criminal agents, the nation and the government of Iran are intimately standing beside you. Since it is a fact that the whole of the Iranian nation is prepared for martyrdom for continuity of our glorious revolution, and will under no circumstances yield to any kind of force and pressure exerted by imperialism and international Zionism, we feel certain that you are also ready for martyrdom alongside your nation and do not accept that the Iranian nation pay ransom to the agents of the world imperialists. You must rest assured that we shall save no effort for your release, and should you so wish and if need be, tens of thousands of Iranians are just ready to enter into the premises of the embassy not with weapons but with cries of "Allaho-Akbar": "God is Great" and thus bring punishment upon these mercenaries of the Ba'athist Iraq in a manner they deserve.

Luckily for the hostages, Ghotbzadeh's plan to invade the embassy with "tens of thousands" of unarmed Iranians was not put into practice. When the time came, the British government chose instead to put its trust in a small number of highly trained, well-armed SAS soldiers.

---

[24]UK Home Office, Siege of the Iranian embassy – "Official History"

5th May 1980: Day 6

By the morning of day six, everyone was tired. The terrorists, particularly Salim, had slept even less than the hostages. The police negotiators, despite working shifts, were also showing the strain. One, unable to cope with the tremendous responsibility, had to be replaced. The others were constantly going over past conversations in their heads, looking for mistakes that they'd made. Professor Gunn, the psychiatrist, spent a lot of time going over recordings with them, reassuring them that they had done well. Neither Professor Gunn nor DAC Dellow expected the siege to end that day, and the uncertainty added to the negotiators' stress. None the less, Dellow was feeling reasonably confident.

At around 04:00, the terrorists woke PC Lock. They were convinced that someone had broken into the embassy on the ground floor, and they sent PC Lock to investigate. He did as he was told, calling out as he went. The noise woke the other hostages, but he found nothing, and so they did their best to get back to sleep.

The terrorists woke the hostages again some hours later. An agitated Salim took PC Lock to the first-floor landing and pointed at a bulge in the plaster. Salim was convinced that the police had removed bricks from the wall so that they could use it as an entry point for an attack. Not knowing the cause of the bulge, PC Lock did his best to calm Salim. Thinking quickly, he told the terrorist leader that if the police did attack, they would not do it during the day. They would do it later, at night. Although both men believed Salim's theory, it seems very unlikely that he was correct. Appendix 2 covers this in more detail.

Ron Morris and Sim Harris set about making breakfast, in what had become something like a routine. There were problems, however: Dr Ezzati was not well, and Salim was getting agitated. He ordered the male hostages moved to the telex room, where they were ordered to sit against the walls. Ominously, the Iranians were kept apart from the others. The atmosphere was extremely tense, with the terrorists holding their weapons at the ready.

In an effort to calm things, Sim Harris and PC Lock managed to persuade a reluctant Salim to let them talk to the police. The police negotiator spoke calmly but offered little of substance. He told them that negotiations were underway, but that the police had no power over such matters. The BBC World Service, he said, would confirm what he had told them.

As they left the talking window, PC Lock tried to persuade Salim against using violence, suggesting that the terrorists should surrender. Salim wouldn't listen. The news from the BBC didn't help; it stated that Arab ambassadors were meeting with COBR, but no final decision had been reached. This wasn't true. In fact, the ambassadors had all refused to help the previous day, but the authorities wanted to give the terrorists some vestige of hope. Unfortunately, it had the opposite effect, finally pushing Salim over the edge. Using the field telephone, he told the negotiator that he would kill a hostage unless he spoke to an ambassador within forty-five minutes.

No ambassador came to the phone, and forty minutes later, the phone rang in Zulu Control. PC Lock, speaking in a calm voice, told the negotiator that the terrorists were tying a hostage to the stairs, and that they were obviously going to shoot him. Salim came on the line, confirming that he would shoot the hostage if his demand was not met. The negotiator didn't budge. He told Salim not to do anything counter-productive. Salim ignored him, and put the hostage on the line. The hostage, Abbas Lavasani, only managed to tell the negotiator his name. Salim shouted at him that he shouldn't have given his name, before taking the phone away.

The police, the SAS, and the hostages all heard the unmistakable sound of three shots being fired. It was 13:45.

Upstairs, the hostages also heard the thud of the body falling. There was stunned silence as they realised what had happened. Some started to cry. When Salim got back to the telex room, he confirmed that Lavasani had been shot. Some of the hostages berated him, but the words fell on deaf ears. He said that he didn't care if the authorities were going to kill him, he was prepared to die. Salim told them that the British government did not care if they lived or died, saying that they would have produced at least one ambassador if they cared. He told the stunned hostages that one of them would be killed every forty-five minutes until he got an answer about the ambassadors.

When they heard the shots, the SAS in the Doctor's House knew that the situation had changed. Although they couldn't be sure that a hostage had been killed, they knew that if someone had been shot, they would be called upon to assault the embassy. Weapons were checked for the umpteenth time, although now with a new sense of urgency.

DAC Dellow and Lieutenant-Colonel Rose believed the shots meant that a hostage had been shot. A dead hostage meant that a peaceful resolution was out of the question. Director de la Billière headed to COBR to report. Whitelaw, the Home Secretary, was at his official residence near Slough. Deciding that his presence was urgently required, he drove to COBR, arriving in just nineteen minutes. He later said that he looked once at the speedometer, and saw that the car was travelling at over 120 miles per hour.

At COBR, de la Billière briefed the assembled officials about the options. A military assault was now the most likely option, and so he talked of the risks involved in such an operation. The plan had been refined over the previous days, but casualties of forty percent among the hostages were still likely. He also emphasised that the decision to deploy the SAS would have to be a political one. If the SAS were to assault, he wanted two hours for final preparations.

At this point, COBR wasn't sure if a hostage had been killed or not. Whitelaw therefore wanted to keep looking for a peaceful solution. With this in mind, the Foreign Secretary, Douglas Hurd, was to contact the friendly Arab ambassadors again. If it became clear that a hostage had been killed, responsibility for concluding the siege would be handed over to the SAS. They were to be ready to attack at short notice. Whitelaw told de la Billière that he would not interfere if the assault did go ahead, but he would accept full responsibility if things went wrong.

The terrorists were persuaded to delay killing the next hostage until 17:00. When de la Billière went to Princes Gate to check on the troops, he found them calm and confident. They knew, but accepted, the risks.

The police had one last idea for a peaceful resolution. They contacted the senior imam at London's Central Mosque, Dr Sayyed Darsh. A superintendent with the anti-terrorist squad knew and respected Dr Darsh. He hoped that Darsh might be willing and able to talk to the terrorists and persuade them to give themselves up. Dr Darsh was reluctant to help, as it would not be compatible with his careful stance of neutrality. However, realising that the siege was unlikely to end peacefully without his help, he agreed to talk to the terrorists. He was rushed to Hyde Park Central police station, and after waiting there for some time, he was taken to Princes Gate itself.

At 16:45, a negotiator contacted the terrorists on the field telephone. He told them that Sir David McNee, the Metropolitan Police Commissioner, had written a letter addressed to them, and that it was very important that they understand it. It had been translated into Farsi, and they wished to arrange for it to be delivered. Salim told them to post it through the letter box, and then told Harris to collect it. PC Lock was held at gunpoint, to be shot if Harris tried anything.

The letter was delivered, with both English and Farsi versions included. It stated that the police were independent of the government, and hoped for a peaceful resolution to the siege. It offered assurances that the police would not resort to violence as long as no hostages were harmed. The letter did not include any offers.

The lack of offers within the letter angered Salim. He told the hostages that another one of them would be killed forty-five minutes later if an ambassador had not arrived.

Meanwhile, Abbas discreetly handed a small piece of paper to Vahid Khabaz, one of the younger hostages. It was a note saying that Abbas wished to run away, and asked for the hostages' help. Khabaz talked to PC Lock, who said that he couldn't guarantee safe passage for Abbas. Lock was wrestling with worries of his own: he'd told Morris that he thought the terrorists would choose him to be the next victim.

The Arab ambassadors who had been contacted by the British government met one final time. They agreed that they would be prepared to help, if certain conditions were met. They wanted a guarantee that there would be no use of force while they negotiated; to be allowed to release a statement that the FCO had asked them for help, not the other way around; and that they were allowed to offer the terrorists safe passage out of the UK if necessary. The British government did not accept the terms. The terrorists would not get their ambassador.

At 18:20, the police made a final, last-ditch attempt to secure a peaceful conclusion. Dr Darsh was taken to the negotiators' room for a final briefing. At this point, he realised that the police simply wanted to use him to secure the terrorists' surrender. He had no power to negotiate. Talking to Salim in Arabic, he told him that he'd heard of the plight of Khuzestan from students at his mosque. Salim angrily told Darsh that he'd killed a hostage already, and he'd kill more unless his demands were met. At 18:41, while Darsh was talking, three gunshots were heard[25]. Salim hung up.

Five minutes later, two men dumped Lavasani's body on the front steps. At 18:49, Salim told a negotiator that one hostage had been killed, and that they would kill another in half an hour. "All the hostages will be killed at once", he said[26].

The police asked for permission to recover the body, and collected it at 18:55[27]. It was immediately obvious that Lavasani had been dead for several hours. Two sets of shots had been heard, though. Did that mean that another hostage was dead inside the embasssy? Salim had said that only one hostage had been killed, but the authorities didn't know if that was true. They assumed two hostages were dead, but it didn't really change anything. One body was enough. The police commissioner rang COBR and told Whitelaw that he wished to commit the SAS. After contacting the prime minister for approval, the home secretary agreed. The decision was made: the siege would not end peacefully.

A call was put in to Saint Stephen's Hospital, alerting them to expect casualties and initiating the Major Accident Procedure. Just

---

[25]UK Home Office, Siege of the Iranian embassy – "Official History"
[26]UK Home Office, Siege of the Iranian embassy – "Official History"
[27]UK Home Office, Siege of the Iranian embassy – "Official History"

before 19:00, Deputy Assistant Commissioner Dellow was about to sign the authority for the SAS to initiate the assault when a garbled call came in. It seemed that the hostages might be released after all. At 19:07, it was finally determined that the hostages were not about to be freed. Dellow signed the document that gave control of the rescue operation to Lieutenant-Colonel Rose. With that signature, the operation came under military command. It was codenamed Operation Nimrod. Major Gullan, Officer Commanding B Squadron, transmitted a message to all SAS troopers that he was in control. Gullan was in a sixth-floor flat with a commanding view of the embassy's rear. The negotiators kept talking to the terrorists, but they changed tactics. Now they were prepared to offer virtually anything, just to keep Salim busy and distracted for as long as possible.

As SAS teams moved into place, the negotiators told Salim that the government had agreed to his demand for a coach to take the terrorists and hostages to a waiting aeroplane. In order to keep him busy and on the phone, the negotiators asked about details. How many seats should the coach have? Where should it park outside the embassy? At this point, they would have agreed to virtually anything to keep Salim on the phone.

At COBR, conversation died down and the room went quiet. There was nothing left to do but wait. Wearing headphones, de la Billière could hear Gullan's commands. Knowing the plan, he was able to give the room a running commentary. Oddly, although most of the country watched the assault live on television, the decision-makers in COBR had to rely on de la Billière's commentary.

THE ASSAULT

The SAS were split into teams with distinct call signs. Juliet One and Two provided sniper support and backup. Two snipers covered the front of the building and four covered the rear. As well as being ready to fire at individual terrorists if the opportunity presented itself, they would provide covering fire and use Polecat grenade launchers to fire gas grenades into the building. Zero Delta would cut off any terrorists who tried to escape, and could also provide covering smoke if needed.

Blue Team and Red Team would perform the assault. Their call signs were Bravo and Romeo, respectively. Each individual sub-unit of two or four was identified by a number (Bravo One, Bravo Two, Romeo One, Romeo Two, etc.). The plan called for everyone to enter simultaneously, with no warning. Every military commander knows the value of surprise. In a hostage-rescue operation, surprise can be the difference between success and catastrophic, bloody failure.

Red Team would take the second, third, and fourth floors of the building. Blue team would take the basement, ground floor, and first floor. Every sub-unit had strictly delineated "limits of exploitation". They would not move beyond these unless absolutely necessary. In the confusion and chaos, these limits would help with command and control, as well as reducing the chances of "friendly fire" incidents. The two teams would meet in the middle of the embassy. To help with identification, each man had a small piece of red or blue coloured tape on his gas mask. Some had also placed coloured tape on their MP5 magazines.

Thirty-two men were to enter the embassy, with another eight deployed to receive hostages at the rear of the building, and four on the roof. The roof men were to provide security and initiate a distraction charge made up of two stun grenades.

Eighteen men from Red Team were to enter from the roof. Four would enter through the skylight to clear the fourth floor. Six more would use ladders to enter the third floor via the light well in the centre of the building. The final eight, Romeo Two, would abseil down the back of the building in two teams of four. They would make entry through the windows on the second-floor balcony, and clear that floor.

Ten men of Blue Team were to enter on the ground floor, through the French windows at the rear. These were call signs Bravo One, Two, and Three. Four of them would clear the basement and secure the stairs. Once that was done, they would form up to receive hostages as they came down the stairs, before passing them on to the reception team outside the rear of the building. The remaining six men were tasked with clearing the ground floor. The final four men of Blue Team, call sign Bravo Four, would enter via the front first-floor balcony, and clear the first floor.

Tensions were high in the Doctor's House. Recognising this, Lance Corporal McAleese held up a novelty cardboard frog. He made croaking noises as he worked a string to make the frog's legs move. The tension was broken as the men burst out laughing at this bizarre sight.

At 19:14, Major Gullan transmitted the code word "Road Accident". This was the signal to start the rescue. Red Team moved onto the embassy roof. The policeman on duty on the roof hadn't been warned to expect black-clad, armed men. After nervously checking with his superiors on the radio, he sensibly retreated to cover. The entry teams moved to their positions while the distraction and security team prepared their charge. Once it was ready, the charge was lowered to just above the glass pyramid in the middle of the second-floor ceiling.

The ten men of Bravo One, Two, and Three moved to their forming-up point, behind a wall at the back of the embassy. Bravo Four were crouched just inside a first-floor balcony of the Doctor's House.

TV news crews had been watching the embassy for days; now their patience paid dividends as they watched the SAS move into position. Their bosses interrupted the normal programming to show the footage live. Luckily there were no televisions switched on inside the embassy. If there had been, the terrorists would have realised a rescue mission was in progress, and all surprise would have been lost.

At 19:23, Gullan transmitted "Hyde Park", the signal for the abseilers to hitch to their ropes, followed closely by "Bank Robbery". The first abseil teams leaned over the edge of the roof, ready to descend. The plan called for Romeo Two to abseil down to the second floor as quickly as possible, then break through the windows. The abseilers wore gloves with reinforced palms, so that they could use their hands to brake. The gloves were too thick to allow a weapon to be used while wearing them. The abseilers wore thinner, Army Air Corps gloves under them, and would remove the abseiling gloves as soon as they landed.

After a few seconds, Gullan transmitted "London Bridge", the code word that indicated the abseilers should start their descent. The abseilers were the first to start the assault, as they needed time to get down to the balcony. Things didn't go well. The leader's rope tangled, and he dangled above the windows, some distance from the balcony, unable to move. The bad luck didn't stop there. On the other rope, Sergeant Tommy Palmer broke a third-floor window with his foot.

Three days before, an SAS trooper had broken a roof tile, but by a stroke of luck the noise hadn't alerted anyone. This time they weren't so lucky. Salim heard the noise of breaking glass. He politely asked the negotiator to stop talking so that he could listen. The negotiator, knowing full well that the rescue mission had started, desperately tried to assure Salim, but to no avail. Salim said that he was going to check, and would be back shortly. PC Lock stayed close as the terrorist headed towards the stairs.

Major Gullan was listening in to the conversation between Salim and the negotiator. When Salim said that he was going to check on the noises, Gullan came to a rapid decision. Foregoing the usual

"Standby, standby" warning order, he immediately transmitted, "Go! Go! Go!" It was 19:24.

Palmer and the other abseilers didn't know if the noise of breaking glass had been heard. They did know that they had to get inside as soon as possible, with or without their leader. Palmer stayed on his rope. He threw a couple of stun grenades through the broken window, then turned to try and help free his leader.

Trooper Collins was with the distraction and security team on the roof. The distraction charge had already been lowered down to the glass pyramid on the second-floor ceiling. On hearing the command, Collins initiated the charge. The blast shook the building as glass shattered, stunning everyone inside. The hope was that the terrorists would look to the source of the blast, in the centre of the building. Thus they would be looking the wrong way when the SAS entered from the front and rear.

GROUND-FLOOR ENTRY

At the rear of the embassy, the men of Bravo One, Two, and Three were in position behind a low wall. The plan was to use a frame charge to blow a way through the French windows. Seeing the stricken abseilers on the second floor and concerned that an explosion would harm them, Lance Corporal Firmin ordered the frame charge removed and made safe. Instead, a sledgehammer was used to break the door lock. A stun grenade was thrown in, swiftly followed by the assault team.

Hassan had fired at the ground-floor entry teams from the second floor, but his shots were wildly inaccurate. The entry teams didn't even realise that they were being fired at[28].

---

[28]Coroner's Report, 3/4 February 1981

First-floor entry

The men of Bravo Four moved onto the first-floor balcony at the front of the Doctor's House. Trooper Parry jumped onto the embassy balcony, closely followed by Lance Corporal McAleese, carrying a frame charge. This was a wooden frame built to fit the target window. Plastic explosive was taped into it, shaped to direct its blast towards the window.

McAleese went to place the frame charge, then stopped as he saw a face on the other side of the window. The face belonged to Sim Harris, whom McAleese recognised as a hostage. McAleese shouted at him to move away from the window and get down, motioning with his hand. Harris, still stunned by the distraction charge, didn't react. Parry joined in, shouting and motioning to Harris to get away from the window. Just as McAleese decided that he had to take the risk of injuring this one hostage in order to rescue the others, Harris understood. He dropped down onto the floor to the side of the window.

McAleese placed the frame charge and secured it, then followed Parry back onto the Doctor's House balcony. McAleese had used the maximum amount of explosive in the frame charge, using the time-honoured formula of "P for Plenty". There was a huge explosion, and a large cloud of smoke obscured the front of the building. McAleese led the men of Bravo Four back onto the embassy balcony. The frame charge had destroyed some of the masonry around the window, as well as the window itself, and the curtains were smouldering. McAleese had probably used more explosive than was strictly necessary, but they had an entry point.

A grenade, dropped by a terrorist in the telex room, landed on the balcony. McAleese stared at it, waiting for it to explode. But the pin was still in place, and it sat there, inert. Presumably the terrorist who dropped it was too excited or nervous to remember to pull the pin out before throwing. Unlike the terrorists, the SAS had received intensive training, and they made few mistakes. They pulled the pins from their own stun grenades before throwing them through the hole where the window had been. As soon as the grenades detonated, the men followed them into the chargé d'affaires' office. The room was clear of terrorists, but they found Sim Harris under a pile of rubble. One of the SAS told Harris to stay where he was until someone came to get him. As two of the sniper team fired CS gas grenades into the building after them, the team headed further into the building.

SECOND-FLOOR ENTRY

On the second floor, two men were now on the balcony, with two stuck on the ropes. The plan had been to use frame charges to blast open the windows, but with the team leader stuck on his rope, that idea was abandoned. Entry tools known as "hooligan bars" were used instead.

Flames flew out of the now-open windows, engulfing the men on the ropes. Realising that the rope couldn't be freed, Palmer abseiled the rest of the way down to the balcony, shouting at the men on the roof to cut the leader's rope. The leader fell about twelve feet, suffering injuries from the fall as well as the burns from the fire. Nonetheless, he stood and joined his team as they all charged through the windows into room nine. Intelligence had said they would find the hostages there. The room was empty. No hostages. No terrorists. No one.

Floor plan: ground floor

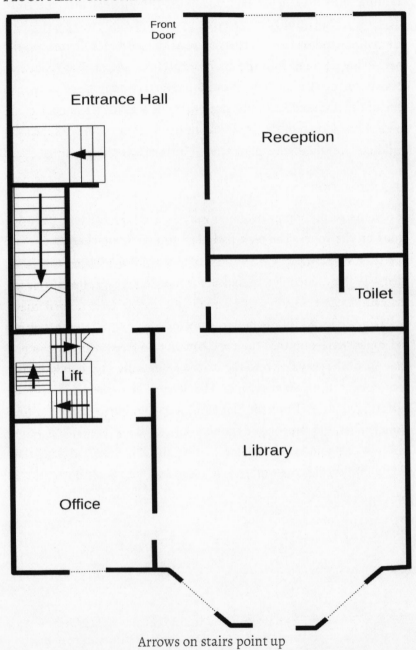

Front Door

Entrance Hall

Reception

Toilet

Lift

Library

Office

Arrows on stairs point up

CLEARING THE GROUND FLOOR

On the ground floor, the SAS entered through the library. The cellar team found the door to the cellar stairs blocked by stepladders. After a quick visual check for booby traps, they moved them out of the way and threw a stun grenade down the stairs. They quickly followed it down and into a corridor. Not having a sledgehammer or shotgun to deal with locked doors, they had to shoot locks with their sub machine guns. Leading the team into the last room, Staff Sergeant Winner thought he saw a figure crouched in a corner. He fired, and as it fell over, he realised he had shot a dustbin.

The ground-floor team cleared their floor, finding no terrorists or hostages. They moved onto the stairs, but stopped at the top, not going onto the landing. This was their limit of exploitation; moving beyond this point without explicit instructions would probably result in being shot by one of their own. The cellar team joined them, forming a line down the stairs and out to the rear lawn. Surviving hostages and terrorists alike would be passed from man to man and then outside, where they would be handcuffed until they had been positively identified. Lance Corporal Firmin positioned himself on the landing half-way up the stairs to the first floor. From here, he would be able to supervise the movement of the hostages from the first floor to the library.

FLOOR PLAN: FIRST FLOOR

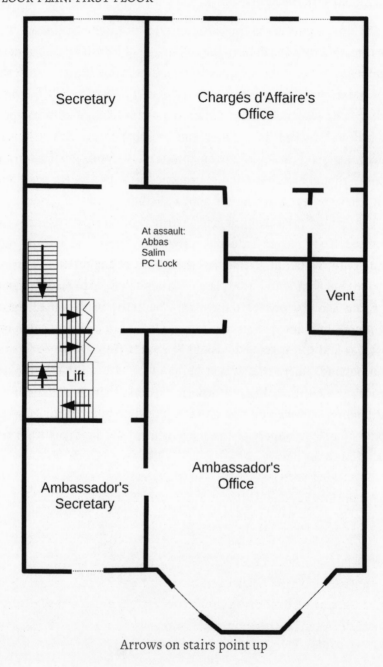

Secretary

Chargés d'Affaire's Office

At assault:
Abbas
Salim
PC Lock

Vent

Lift

Ambassador's Office

Ambassador's Secretary

Arrows on stairs point up

CLEARING THE FIRST FLOOR

PC Lock had stayed close to Salim, and when the distraction charge was detonated, he realised that an assault was in progress. Lock shoulder-charged the terrorist leader, knocking him into the office of the chargés d'affaire's secretary. Salim dropped his Skorpion submachine gun. He tried to pick it up, but Lock knocked him to the floor. As the two men grappled on the floor, Lock drew his revolver.

The four men who had entered through the first-floor balcony at the front now split into two pairs. Macdonald and Deggs went out onto the first-floor landing, while Parry and McAleese checked the small room to the left of the door. Finding it clear, they headed for the first-floor landing to meet the other two.

Macdonald and Deggs had gone straight to the office next door, where they found PC Lock and Salim struggling on the floor. Recognising the policeman, they shouted "Trevor! Roll clear!" One of them pushed Lock away, and on seeing that Salim had a weapon, both fired, hitting him in the head and chest. They helped Lock, who was obviously suffering from exposure to CS gas, to a window to get some fresh air. Once recovered, he told them that there were six terrorists. This was useful information, and one of the team leaned out of the door to shout, "PC confirms: six terrorists". Then they helped Lock out to the stairs, where SAS troopers passed him from one to another until he was outside on the rear lawn.

Abbas was spotted in the doorway of the ambassador's office, at the rear of the building. Deggs fired at him. Wounded, Abbas ducked back into the room. None of Bravo Four had a light on their MP5s, so they took a man from the stairs who did. Deggs kept watch on the landing as the others followed a stun grenade into the ambassador's office. Advancing cautiously, they found the wounded terrorist at the rear of the room. He had a Browning automatic pistol in his hand. As he started to lift the pistol, all four men fired at him from a range of just a few yards.

Parry and McAleese went back into the chargés d'affaire's office and moved Harris onto the balcony. They instructed him to stay there, then moved back into the body of the building. Seeing that the fire was getting worse, Harris started to get up, but a voice from outside the building shouted at him to get down. A little later, Parry and McAleese went back for him, but the fire in the room was too fierce. They moved into the adjacent secretary's office and went out of the window onto the balcony. They shouted at Harris to jump over to their balcony. He jumped, and they helped him back inside, then threw him into the chain that was moving hostages out of the rear of the building.

FLOOR PLAN: SECOND FLOOR

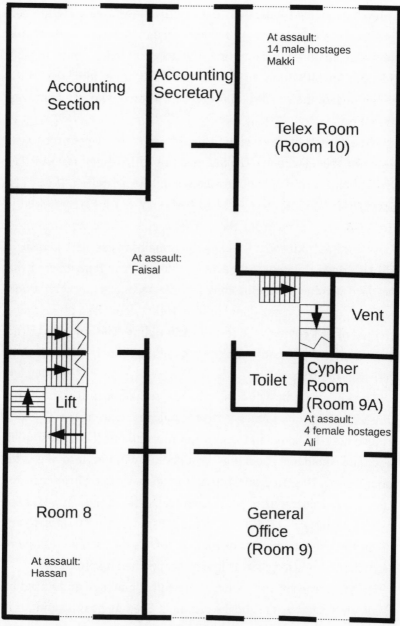

Accounting Section

Accounting Secretary

At assault:
14 male hostages
Makki

Telex Room
(Room 10)

At assault:
Faisal

Vent

Toilet

Cypher
Room
(Room 9A)
At assault:
4 female hostages
Ali

Lift

Room 8

At assault:
Hassan

General
Office
(Room 9)

Arrows on stairs point up

CLEARING THE SECOND FLOOR

Intelligence had indicated that the male hostages were in room nine, and the female hostages were in the cypher room, 9A, a small room that led off from room nine. The door was locked, but a burst of fire from an MP5 soon dealt with that. This time, intelligence was correct: inside the small room were four women, two of whom were screaming.

If the male hostages weren't in room nine, they were probably in room ten, the telex room. The SAS had to get there, and fast. Another door led out of room nine onto the second-floor landing. It was also locked, but even after the lock had been shot out it barely moved. It had been barricaded from the opposite side. There were no other doors leading from room nine. As the remaining abseilers joined the effort to open the door, Sergeant Tommy Palmer remembered that the third window on the balcony led to a second room, with a door leading onto the second-floor landing. If that door wasn't barricaded, it would offer a route to the rest of the building. The only way to that room was via the balcony, and the back of the room and the windows were well and truly ablaze.

Palmer chose the window with the smaller bonfire and threw himself through the flames, onto the balcony. Once there he had to remove his NBC hood and respirator and slap out the flames on his head and shoulders. Looking through the window into the other room, he saw Hassan crouching on the floor. Without his respirator, Palmer could clearly smell petrol, and realised that Hassan was trying to set the rug on fire. He raised his MP5, aimed it at Hassan, and pulled the trigger. Instead of the roar of a sub machine gun being fired, there was just a click. Palmer's weapon had misfired.

Hassan turned at the sound, dropped his matches, and raised his pistol. He fired, but the shots went high. Even as he was doing this, Palmer was dropping his MP5 and drawing his backup pistol, but

Hassan had run out of the room by the time the pistol was drawn. Palmer gave chase, and Hassan ran to the telex room, where gunshots and screams could be clearly heard.

Red Team's delay getting into the building had given the terrorists a little time to react. When the assault started, there were four terrorists on the second floor. Makki was in the telex room, where the male hostages were sitting on the floor. Ali was guarding the female hostages in the cipher room. Hassan and Faisal were also on that floor.

After the distraction charge was detonated, Ali left the women and moved to the telex room to join Makki, followed by Faisal. Realising that they were under attack, they started shooting wildly into the press of hostages. Ali Akbar Samadzadeh, the assistant press attaché, was hit by two bullets and died immediately. Dr Afrouz was hit in the face and legs. Ahmed Dadgar was hit in the chest, back, arms, and legs, suffering serious wounds. Two other hostages were remarkably lucky. Ali Aghar Tabatabai felt the passage of a bullet passing him, but wasn't hit. A bullet struck Abbas Fallahi on the hip, but bounced off a fifty-pence coin, leaving him merely bruised.

Hassan ran into the telex room, pulling out a grenade. The other three terrorists lost their nerve, dropping their guns and mingling with the hostages on the floor. Hassan remained standing. When Palmer burst into the room, he saw that Hassan had a grenade in his hand, and that he was moving to pull the pin. Palmer fired a single shot, which hit Hassan in the head and killed him instantly. The rest of the second-floor team entered, having forced their way out of room nine.

As they applied quick first aid to the wounded hostages, the SAS recognised Makki as a terrorist. He was ordered to lie face down on the floor, with his arms outstretched in a T shape. As he was being checked for weapons, he pulled his arms in towards his body and started to turn over. Believing that he was going for a grenade, the team leader shot him with his MP5.

EVACUATION

The SAS started to move the men out of the telex room and to the stairs. Realising that two terrorists were still unaccounted for, the SAS almost threw the men from one soldier to the next. This ensured that they kept moving, and also made it harder for the remaining terrorists to take the initiative and act aggressively.

As the hostages moved down the stairs, Lance Corporal McAleese recognised Faisal, one of the terrorists. He shouted a warning to the men on the stairs, lifting his respirator to make himself heard more clearly. Faisal received a number of kicks and punches as he was bundled down the stairs. As he drew level with Staff Sergeant Winner, the SAS man saw a grenade in the terrorist's hand. He moved to shoot, but realised that there was a strong possibility that the bullets would pass through Faisal and hit hostages, or his colleagues. Instead, he raised the MP5 over his head and brought the butt of the weapon down on the terrorist's head. Faisal rolled down the remaining stairs, landing on the ground-floor carpet. Four submachine guns fired, and he was hit thirty-nine times. As Firmin checked his pulse, someone yelled a warning: "Grenade!" It had rolled out of Faisal's dead hand. For a moment, Firmin thought he was a dead man. Then he breathed a sigh of relief. The pin hadn't been pulled out. The grenade was safe.

When the last of the hostages had exited the building, an order came over the radio for the SAS to get out. The embassy was now burning fiercely on the upper floors. They exited through the library and turned left, heading back to the Doctor's House. There, they removed their body armour and relaxed.

As the hostages exited the library, the reception team of SAS and police took over. Each person was handcuffed and placed on the grass, face down. PC Lock, still in his uniform, was the only exception. This treatment was designed to ensure that no terrorists escaped in the confusion. Once they were all safely cuffed, the reception team worked to identify them. Ali, the only surviving terrorist, tried to claim that he was a student, but Sim Harris recognised him and gave him away. A pair of uniformed policemen escorted him to a waiting police van, which took him to Paddington Green police station. He was interrogated later that night.

Now that everyone was out, control passed back from military to civilian hands. The fire brigade were allowed to start fighting the fire. By this time it had taken a strong hold over the upper floors of the building, and it did a great deal of damage to the embassy and adjoining buildings before being put out.

At the Doctor's House, police officers handed plastic bags to the SAS. Their weapons, labelled to identify the user, were placed into these bags for later forensic examination. Investigators would match the wounds on the terrorists to individual soldiers' weapons. Five terrorists and one hostage had been killed during the assault, and the police intended to determine whether or not the SAS had acted within the law. Although they had entered the building heavily armed, with every expectation of using their weapons to kill, every death had to be investigated. The SAS are not a death squad; even in the extreme situation of the Iranian embassy, they were expected to operate within the law.

The soldiers themselves wanted to know who had won the snooker tournament they'd been watching, which had been close to a finish when the assault started. Most of them wanted Alex Higgins to win, and so were disappointed to learn that Higgins had lost to Cliff Thorburn. A greater surprise was the revelation that the BBC had interrupted coverage of the snooker final to show live footage of the assault. None of them had been aware that the assault was being filmed, let alone that it was broadcast live.

At COBR, de la Billière was able to report that the assault had been a success. The silence was replaced with talking, shouting, and laughing. Papers flew into the air and bottles of whisky appeared. Shortly after, Whitelaw and de la Billière headed to Princes Gate, where they congratulated John Dellow and Mike Rose. Then they moved on to Regent's Park Barracks, where the assault teams had been discreetly moved.

Hostage Debriefing

The hostages were all loaded onto ambulances and taken to Saint Stephen's Hospital, where the Accident and Emergency department had been cleared, ready for their arrival. Most hostages had only minor injuries, but Dr Afrouz and Dadgar had more serious gunshot wounds. Dadgar had to be taken to the intensive care unit, but he and Afrouz both made a full recovery.

Much to their surprise, with the exception of PC Trevor Lock, once the rest of the hostages had been treated they were moved onto a coach and taken to Hendon Police College. Despite protests, they were not allowed to contact anyone. They were fed and given a sedative to help them sleep, but they still weren't allowed to make contact with the outside world. The next day involved several hours of debriefing, during which Harris realised that there was some thought that he and Cramer had forewarning of the terrorists' attack. It must have looked suspicious that a BBC news team was on the premises at the moment that the terrorists struck. As Harris pointed out, their presence did the terrorists little good. Since they were only there to get visas, they had no recording equipment with them. Once the police were satisfied that they had everything they needed, all of the hostages were allowed to go.

SAS Debriefing

Once their weapons had been given to the police, and they had got changed, the SAS were moved to Regent's Park Barracks in unmarked vehicles. There they found crates of lager, and the men and officers stood around chatting and drinking. They were joined by the Prime Minister, Margaret Thatcher, and her husband Denis. The prime minister gave a speech, in which she congratulated and thanked the men. Then she and her husband moved around the room, speaking to each man individually. Denis Thatcher allegedly complained to one soldier that they had "let one of the bastards live"[29].

A television was wheeled into the room in time for the BBC Nine O'Clock News. As it started, a voice from the back of the room shouted for the person at the front to sit down so that others could see. Mrs Thatcher obediently sat on the floor.

The next day, detectives arrived at SAS headquarters in Hereford. They were there to do an extensive debrief with the assault teams. They took statements, and recorded where and when every shot had been fired. This had been practiced many times during exercises over the years, so the soldiers were prepared and knew what was expected of them. Nonetheless, the process took thirty-six hours to complete.

---

[29]SAS: Embassy Siege, broadcast on BBC2, 2002

Aftermath

The Iraqi news agency in London filed an account of the assault that was critical of the way the siege ended. The account was reported by the Al Iraq newspaper in Iraq[30]. Headlined "British Plot Ends in Storming of the Persian Regime's London Embassy", it stated that "provocation by the British authorities" led to the "martyrdom" of members of the group. It even went so far as to claim that a British police spokesman had "admitted this provocation when he explained that his police team had sought the assistance of a unit of the SAS with the agreement of William Whitelaw, the Home Secretary, to storm the embassy at a time when negotiations were still going on between the two sides".

In Iran, on the other hand, the British embassy reported that "There is widespread admiration here, both in the street and from government officials with whom we have been in contact, for the decisive action taken to end the siege"[31]. Bani Sadr sent a message to Mrs Thatcher expressing gratitude for the "persevering action of your police force that proved its competence during the unjust hostage-

---

[30]TNA: FCO 8/3660
[31]TNA: FCO 8/3660

taking event at the Iranian embassy in London and the lives of all but one of our very dear children were saved in this event"[32]. Even in Iran there was some discontent. The Islamic Republic newspaper continued to claim that the CIA, British intelligence, and British police were involved in the hostage-taking.

Ali, real name Fowzi Badavi Nejad, was held in Brixton prison to await his trial. He had assumed that he would be given a summary trial leading to a quick conviction. It came as something of a shock to find that solicitors had been appointed to help with his defence[33] He was also pleasantly surprised by the humane conditions in which he was detained. His trial was held at the Old Bailey, where he was charged with murder, conspiracy to murder, unlawful imprisonment and possessing firearms with intent[34]. He pleaded not guilty to murder, and guilty to the other charges. Later, the Crown accepted a plea of guilty to manslaughter in lieu of the murder charge. He was sentenced to life imprisonment, with a minimum term of twenty-five years. Passing sentence, Justice Sir Hugh Park told him that he had taken part in an "outrageous criminal enterprise", and caused "unspeakable terror, anguish, and distress".

A coroner's inquiry was held to determine the cause of death of each of the terrorists. The jury returned unanimous verdicts of justifiable homicide in all cases. Section 3 of the Criminal Law Act 1967 provides that a person may "use such force as is reasonable in the circumstances in the prevention of crime, or in effecting or assisting in the lawful arrest of offenders or suspected offenders"[35]. The coroner opined in his report that Faisal and Makki need not have died. If Makki had not appeared to reach for a grenade, and Faisal

---

[32]TNA: FCO 8/3660
[33]TNA: FCO 8/3661
[34]TNA: J 267/864
[35]Criminal Law Act 1967, part 1, section 3

had not brandished a grenade on the stairs, both of them would have survived.

There was some controversy over the deaths of Faisal and Hassan. One of the hostages, Mr Fallahi, claimed that an SAS soldier had held Hassan's head under his arm and shot him at point-blank range. However, the evidence of both the ballistics expert and the forensic pathologist contradicted this claim. The coroner reminded the jury that Fallahi's evidence had been confused, and that even with an interpreter, there had been language difficulties. Initially, one hostage, Mr Tabatabai, appeared to claim that he had seen Faisal shot in the back of the head at point-blank range, in the telex room. He later said that he'd seen Faisal being held by his hair, but hadn't seen how or where he had died.

PC Lock was awarded the George Medal for displaying "gallantry and devotion to duty of an extremely high order when in spite of the long strain and ordeal of his capture, he tackled and overpowered this dangerous and armed man who had already caused the death of one hostage". The citation credited PC Lock with saving the lives of hostages, stating that "on more than one occasion when, but for his intervention, the hostages' lives might have been lost"[36].

Historically, the SAS had always shunned publicity. Although deployments had been publicly announced on occasion, most of the general public knew very little about them. The live television coverage of the embassy assault thrust them into public view, and in a very positive way. The IRA in Northern Ireland had been running a negative-publicity campaign against the SAS; the embassy assault negated much of the IRA's efforts.

The two territorial army SAS regiments, 21 SAS and 23 SAS, found themselves inundated with recruits. Many of them, in the words of de la Billière, were "convinced that a balaclava helmet and a Heckler & Koch submachine gun would be handed to them over the counter, so

---

[36]Recorded in The Gazette (London Gazette), issue 48584, 13 April 1981

that they could go off and conduct embassy-style sieges of their own"[37].

There was a great deal of national pride in the wake of the assault. The SAS's expertise and knowledge became keenly sought after, with various foreign governments requesting help to train their own hostage-rescue and special forces units.

The SAS, for their part, learned some valuable lessons from the operation. The assault equipment was improved. Fire-resistant clothing was introduced, and greater numbers of integrated weapon torches were procured. The success at Princes Gate meant that funding for new hostage-rescue equipment was easy to obtain.

Both the police and the SAS received a lot of praise, and it was well-deserved. The police gave very little to the terrorists, yet secured the release of several hostages. International experience had shown that patient, gradual wearing down of the terrorists offered the best chance of a peaceful resolution. The British police had experience of hostage-takers, but in previous instances the taking of hostages wasn't pre-planned; it was done as a last resort. The Iranian embassy was different. The terrorists had attacked with the specific intention of securing hostages. Still, the police weren't entirely clueless. Police and anti-terrorist agencies in various Western countries routinely shared intelligence and techniques for dealing with terrorist attacks of all kinds. Although this was the first time terrorists had taken hostages and issued demands in Britain, other countries had experience of this type of incident, and their knowledge was freely shared. The tactics that the British police used were a result of the experiences of all these organisations. They offered the best chance of a peaceful conclusion.

With the benefit of hindsight, it can be difficult to remember that hostage rescues like Operation Nimrod are risky affairs, with no

---

[37]Looking for Trouble: SAS to Gulf Command: the Autobiography, Peter de la Billière, HarperCollins, 1995, ISBN 978-0-00-637983-6

certainty of success. Operation Eagle Claw, the US attempt to rescue hostages from their embassy in Iran, had failed just ten days before. That failure was prominent in the minds of the decision-makers when they decided to commit the SAS. It is a testament to the training and professionalism of the SAS that they were able to conduct a rescue in such a large, sprawling building, with only one death among the hostages. Their intense training meant that they were able to overcome problems such as one abseiler getting caught on his rope, and the same team finding a door locked and barricaded.

If the assault had gone wrong, the reaction would have been very different. The Iranian government could have used Bromley's letter to Afrouz as evidence that the police had underestimated the risk to the embassy. Diplomatic relations between Britain and Iran were already cool following the overthrow of the shah and the ongoing hostage crisis in the US embassy. A failed rescue would have had a further chilling effect. As it was, the Iranian government claimed compensation from the British government, claiming that the British had violated Article 22 of the 1961 Vienna Convention on Diplomatic Relations[38], which states:

> "The receiving State is under a special duty to take all appropriate steps to protect the premises of the mission against any intrusion or damage and to prevent any disturbance of the peace of the mission or impairment of its dignity".

Iran claimed that Britain had failed in this obligation, saying that they had repeatedly raised concerns about security at the embassy, but that these had not been taken seriously. In failing to discharge their "special duty", the British government had "caused the intrusion of the armed terrorists into the premises of the chancery of this embassy"[39]. Particular reference was made to Bromley's letter, which

---

[38]Vienna Convention on Diplomatic Relations, 1961, article 22
[39]TNA: FCO 8/4102

had arrived the day before the attack. The Iranian government claimed that despite their concerns, "no appropriate step was taken by the British Government to prevent the armed intrusion of the terrorists into the premises of the chancery of this embassy"[40].

The British position was that they had no legal obligation to pay compensation. They believed they had taken all appropriate steps. They noted that the DPG had repeatedly advised the Iranians to install "air lock" style security doors, but this recommendation had not been acted upon[41]. The warning that Bromley had responded to immediately before the attack had been very vague. Eventually Iran and Britain agreed to mutual compensation. Britain paid compensation to Iran for the damage done in London, while Iran paid Britain for the damage done to the British embassy in Tehran during the 1979 Islamic Revolution.

The Ethiopian government also claimed compensation for damage to their embassy, which was adjacent to the Iranian embassy. Police had not occupied the embassy during the siege[42], but the building had suffered damage, primarily from the fires that started during the SAS assault. The police had not allowed the fire brigade to enter the premises until they could be sure that no terrorists remained inside, and this delay had exacerbated the damage.

Some in the British government thought that the Ethiopians were taking advantage of the situation to improve the embassy at British expense. The condition before the siege was described by one civil servant as "extremely shabby". The Ethiopian ambassador had to seek alternative accommodation in a hotel until the damage was repaired, moving back in on 6th August. The British government eventually paid £50,000 for repairs, cleaning, and accommodation.

---

[40]TNA: FCO 8/4102
[41]TNA: FCO 8/4102
[42]TNA: FCO 31/2809

In October 2008, after serving 28 years, Fowzi Nejad was freed on parole. The Iranian government strongly condemned the decision, and called for him to be deported to Iran[43]. The British government refused, on the grounds that he was likely to be executed by the Iranian authorities.

---

[43]Reuters, 11 October 2008

Appendix 1: Weapons and Equipment

HECKLER & KOCH MP5 SUBMACHINE GUN

The German Heckler & Koch MP5 was the standard submachine gun used by the CRW. It has a well-deserved reputation for reliability and accuracy, both of which are very important during a hostage-rescue operation. The magazine holds thirty rounds of standard NATO 9mm pistol ammunition.

The MP5 is available in several variants. Although most troopers involved in Operation Nimrod used the standard model, a few had the MP5SD model, with an in-built silencer. Some of the MP5s also had torches mounted above the barrel. As well as the standard and silenced versions, the SAS train on the MP5K, a shortened version often used in bodyguarding work.

L9A1 BROWNING HI-POWER PISTOL

The L9A1 Browning Hi-Power was the standard British Army pistol in 1980, and every SAS trooper on hostage-rescue duties carried one in a thigh holster, for use as a backup weapon. The magazine holds thirteen rounds. Like the MP5, it fires standard NATO 9mm ammunition.

The terrorists also had four Browning Hi-Power pistols, loaded with Winchester hollow-point ammunition.

L74A1 Remington 870 Shotgun

A 12-gauge pump-action shotgun. Used by the SAS primarily for shooting locks and hinges, thus allowing quick entry through locked doors. The magazine holds seven rounds.

Skorpion Vz. 61 Submachine Gun

The Skorpion is a Czech-designed submachine gun. It fires 7.65mm ammunition from ten or twenty-round magazines. Small and compact, with a folding stock, it is relatively easy to conceal, making it popular among terrorists.

.38 Smith & Wesson Revolver

PC Lock carried a standard-issue .38 Smith & Wesson Model 10 revolver, and the terrorists also had one. The Model 10 was widely used by police forces and the military, until automatic pistols became more widespread. It carries six rounds in a revolving cylinder.

G60 Stun Grenade

Stun grenades, also known as "flash-bang" grenades, were developed by the SAS during the 1970s, and were first used at Mogadishu in 1977. Unlike standard grenades, they are not designed to wound or kill. Instead, they produce an extremely bright flash and loud noise. Most effective in an enclosed space, such as a room, they will disorientate people in their vicinity for a short time without causing permanent damage. This means that they can be used to temporarily incapacitate hostage-takers without harming the hostages.

CS Gas Grenade

A complement to the stun grenades, CS gas (tear gas) grenades can help to neutralise hostage-takers, without causing permanent harm to any hostages. CS gas is an irritant, and causes burning in the eyes, nose, and throat. The victim will find it difficult to keep their eyes open, and both the eyes and nose will run profusely.

RGD-5 Hand Grenade

The terrorists had several Soviet-made RGD-5 hand grenades. This was the standard Soviet army anti-personnel fragmentation grenade for some years, and was widely exported, including to Iraq. It produces around 350 fragments, with a lethality radius of twenty-five metres, making it a powerful weapon in an enclosed space such as a room.

Frame Charge

A wooden frame with an explosive charge fitted to it, with the blast's force directed away from the frame. They are used to blow holes in walls, doors, or armoured glass. In Operation Nimrod the plan was to use them at all three entry points, but only the front one was used because of the risk to the abseiler stuck on his rope.

Sledgehammer

The SAS can call upon a variety of highly advanced equipment, but sometimes it fails to work or cannot be used. At those times, something as simple as a sledgehammer can be invaluable. During Operation Nimrod, one entry team used a sledgehammer to smash open a door, since using frame charges would have put one of their comrades at risk.

HOOLIGAN BAR

Another low-tech entry device, the hooligan bar comes in several lengths, from 24" to 42". All models are made of alloy steel and are double-ended, with a claw for prying open, a spike, and a wedge. This combination of tools means that virtually any door or window can be forced open.

BODY ARMOUR

In 1980, British Army soldiers did not normally wear body armour. In hostage-rescue situations, however, body armour was a standard part of the SAS trooper's equipment. The body armour worn consisted of a Kevlar vest and heavy ballistic plates. Although Kevlar is effective at stopping shrapnel and low-velocity pistol rounds, it is much less effective at stopping high-velocity rounds, such as those fired by rifles. The ballistic plates provide a high level of protection against high-velocity rounds.

S6 RESPIRATOR

The SAS use the standard British Army S6 respirator. CRW teams train to mount rescue operations whilst wearing the respirator. Speed and surprise are important during hostage-rescue operations. There is no time to put a respirator on during an operation, so the troopers wear it as standard.

Appendix 2: The Wall

On the last day of the siege, Salim noticed a bulge in the wall separating the Iranian and Ethiopian embassies and pointed it out to PC Lock. Both Salim and Lock believed that the police had tampered with the wall, weakening it in order to use it as an entry point for an assault. This claim appears to have originally gained credibility in the book Siege! Princes Gate, London – The Great Embassy Rescue[44], published in 1980. The authors state that workmen removed bricks from the wall to facilitate placement of pinhole cameras for surveillance. Other books and articles claim that a large number of bricks were removed, leaving just a thin layer of plaster, so that the SAS could burst through the walls and into the embassy. The only evidence for these claims appears to be PC Lock's testimony. It must be remembered that after six days as a hostage, he was tired and emotionally overwrought. There is no reason to doubt the existence of a bulge in the plaster, but there is evidence to suggest that it was not caused by the removal of bricks from the wall.

---

[44]Siege! Princes Gate, London – The Great embassy Rescue, Sunday Times "Insight" Team, Times Newspapers Ltd, 1980 ISBN 0-600-20337-9

Two days after the assault, the Metropolitan Police Headquarters Surveyor submitted a report detailing damage to the Ethiopian embassy as a result of the siege[45]. The report notes that there was no police occupation of the embassy during the siege. It makes no mention of bricks missing from walls, or of holes in the wall adjoining the Iranian embassy. An official from the Ethiopian embassy was present during the survey. Note that the Ethiopians had a vested interest in making sure that all damage was included, since they were pressuring the UK government for compensation.

It would be extremely difficult to remove the bricks from one side of a wall whilst retaining the plaster on the far side. It might be possible, if the plaster had already separated from the bricks on the Iranian side, but even then it would be difficult. Having no access to the Iranian side of the wall, the police wouldn't have been able to determine whether or not the plaster had separated. If it hadn't, large holes would have appeared in the wall when the bricks were removed, with disastrous effects.

If, as some accounts claim, enough bricks had been removed to allow entry through the wall, why wasn't it used? In hostage-rescue operations speed and surprise are critical to success. Speaking of the plan, de la Billière said himself, "The essence of it was speed and surprise"[46]. Going through the wall would have provided fast entry into the heart of the building, close to where the hostages were held, without the potential problem of barricaded doors.

Several first-hand accounts by SAS veterans of the siege have been published, and none of the veterans mention an attempt to remove bricks from walls in order to gain an additional entry point. Nor is it mentioned in General (then Brigadier) Sir Peter de la Billière's memoirs.

---

[45]TNA: FCO 31/2809

[46]Looking for Trouble: SAS to Gulf Command: the Autobiography, Peter de la Billière, HarperCollins, 1995, ISBN 978-0-00-637983-6

Finally, at least one source claims that bricks were removed by army engineers[47], not council workmen. Although this is a small discrepancy, it does add to the general weight of evidence.

It is, of course, notoriously difficult to prove a negative. Nonetheless, the above evidence strongly suggests that this is an urban myth, and that no bricks were removed from the wall between the Iranian and Ethiopian embassies.

[47]Who Dares Wins - The SAS and the Iranian Embassy Siege 1980, Gregory Fremont-Barnes, Osprey Publishing, 2012, ISBN 978-1-78096-468-3

Glossary

Chargé d'Affaires: The head of an embassy, where the embassy does not have an ambassador.

COBR (pronounced "cobra"): Cabinet Office Briefing Room, the British national crisis office.

CRW: Counter-Revolutionary Warfare wing. The division of 22nd SAS Regiment tasked with training the sabre squadrons in anti-terrorist and hostage-rescue operations.

D Notice: An official request from the British government to the press and media, asking them not to report on a particular issue that could jeopardise national security. Compliance was voluntary, but it was unusual for a news outlet to ignore one.

DA plan: Deliberate Action plan. A more detailed plan than the Immediate Action plan, making use of all available intelligence.

DAC: Deputy Assistant Commissioner. A senior rank in the Metropolitan Police Force.

DPG: Diplomatic Protection Group. The branch of the British police charged with protecting diplomatic premises and people.

FCO: British Foreign and Commonwealth Office.

Frame charge: An explosive charge mounted in a wooden frame, to be positioned against a door or window. When detonated, it blows a hole in the door or window.

Hooligan bar: A tool used for forcing entry through a door or window.

IA plan: Immediate Action plan. A hastily drawn-up plan, which is put into action if required before the Deliberate Action plan is ready.

Killing House: A specially-outfitted building at SAS headquarters, used for close-quarter combat and hostage-rescue training.

MACP: Military Aid to the Civil Power. The British legal framework that allows the armed forces to provide assistance (armed if necessary) to the police and government.

MBS: Main Base Station. The primary location from which an operation is conducted.

MOD: British Ministry of Defence.

Note verbale: An unsigned diplomatic note.

Sabre squadron: SAS combat squadron. The SAS has four sabre squadrons, designated A, B, D, and G.

SP Team: Special Projects Team. The SAS squadron currently assigned to anti-terrorist duties. Formerly known as "Pagoda Troop".

Digital Reinforcements: Free Ebook

To get a free ebook of this title, simply go to www.shilka.co.uk/dr and enter code NIMROD17.

The free ebook can be downloaded in several formats: Mobi (for Kindle devices & apps), ePub (for other ereaders & ereader apps), and PDF (for reading on a computer). Ereader apps are available for all computers, tablets and smartphones.

About Russell Phillips

Russell Phillips writes books and articles about military technology and history. His articles have been published in Miniature Wargames, Wargames Illustrated and the Society of Twentieth Century Wargamers' Journal. Some of these articles are available on his website.

To get a free book and advance notice of new books, join Russell's mailing list at www.rpbook.co.uk/freebook. You can unsubscribe at any time.

Word of mouth is crucial for any author to succeed. If you enjoyed this book, please consider leaving a review where you bought it, or on a site like Goodreads. Even a short review would be very much appreciated.

ALSO BY RUSSELL PHILLIPS

Red Steel: Soviet Tanks and Combat Vehicles of the Cold War

This We'll Defend: The Weapons and Equipment of the U.S. Army

A Fleet in Being: Austro-Hungarian Warships of WWI

A Damn Close-Run Thing: A Brief History of the Falklands War

The Bear Marches West: 12 Scenarios for 1980s NATO vs Warsaw Pact Wargames

FIND RUSSELL PHILLIPS ONLINE

Website: www.rpbook.co.uk
Twitter: @RPBook
Facebook: facebook.com/RussellPhillipsBooks
Google Plus: google.com/+RussellPhillips
E-mail: russell@rpbook.co.uk
Join Russell's mailing list: www.rpbook.co.uk/freebook

Printed in Great Britain
by Amazon